KING ALFRED'S COLLEGE

The Technological Classroom

A BLUEPRINT FOR SUCCESS

The Technological Classroom

A BLUEPRINT FOR SUCCESS

Ann Heide

Dale Henderson

Trifolium Books Inc.
TORONTO, CANADA

Irwin Publishing
TORONTO, CANADA

Trifolium Books Inc.
238 Davenport Road, Suite 28
Toronto, Ontario, Canada M5R 1J6

Exclusive distribution in Canada
IRWIN PUBLISHING
1800 Steeles Avenue West
Concord, Ontario, Canada L4K 2P3

Canadian Cataloguing in Publication Data

Heide, Ann, 1948-
   The technological classroom : a blueprint for success

Includes bibliographical references.
In Canada: ISBN 0-7725-2141-7

1. Educational technology. 2. Audio-visual
education. I. Henderson, Dale, 1948-
II. Title.

LB1043.H45 1994   371.3'3   C94-931466-8

Editor: June Trusty
Project coordinator: Diane Klim
Production coordinator: Francine Geraci
Design and artwork: Julian Cleva
Cartoons and artwork: Larry Stewart
Artwork on pages 18 and 105: Petra Bockus

Printed and bound in Canada
   96 97 98 9 8 7 6 5 4 3

Contents

Acknowledgments

We sincerely thank the many individuals and organizations who made this endeavor possible:

- The Carleton Roman Catholic School Board for use of curriculum materials;
- The Ottawa Board of Education for use of Track 21 materials;
- Doug, Brett, and Kerri Henderson for their patience, understanding, and support over many long months;
- Jim Rogerson for encouraging us to write this book;
- Trudy Rising, Mary Kay Winter, Grace Deutsch, and June Trusty for their mentoring of novice authors, encouragement, help, and honest advice;
- Sandy Nishikawa of Regent Park Public School, Nola McIntyre of Sprucecourt Public School, and Dace Phillips of Bell Canada, for their thorough and extremely helpful reviews;
- Larry Stewart, artist, and Paul Telfer, photographer, for contributing their creativity and talent;
- Christine Chapman, without whose computer expertise we would have struggled for endless hours with figures and diagrams;
- Elizabeth Klassen and Debbi Wensley for continually adding to our computer skills, helping with technology, and reviewing our work in progress;
- Sharron Anderson, Eleanor Bellefeuille, Laurie DiLabio, Danuta Dynowski-Horan, Sonja Karsh, Alana Morris, Bev Murphy, Carole Parent, Jim Rogers, and Sandra Tischer, for providing their "real-life" experiences with technology in their classrooms and schools;
- Dorothy Collins and Paul Gibson for taking the time to give us valuable feedback as our work progressed;
- Experienced technicians Randy Fitton and Peter Wellington, who readily shared their expertise;
- The many students who allowed us to photograph them at work with technology.

Ann Heide and Dale Henderson

Preface

The longest journey begins with a single step.
(Chinese proverb)

Five years ago, a school board embarked on an ambitious project: designing and implementing a curriculum that not only integrated technology into the daily experiences of students, but also embodied the best of current educational techniques. After visiting schools across North America, the developers at the Carleton Roman Catholic School Board, located near Ottawa, Canada, began to plan a model, a model that has undergone many significant changes since its inception and continues to evolve as society and needs change. Equipment was purchased, curriculum was rewritten, and teachers were trained. From one pilot classroom, this program has expanded over five years to encompass all classes for students aged 9 through 16 and to win international acclaim.

During these years, we have shared the responsibility for this educational innovation with other dedicated professionals in our school system. Through our experience in growing with this project, we learned a great deal about creating technology-integrated classrooms and about the change process. This book combines the collective thoughts of researchers and theorists with the dreams, experiences, ideas, and concerns of the many educators with whom we have had the privilege to work.

In the process of our introducing technology-integrated classrooms, we have learned much from both students and teachers. Among the lessons learned from the students, perhaps the most important was never to underestimate their ability to work with technology and to discover new and better ways of using it. Added to this, the enthusiasm and hard work of the teachers transformed concepts into reality in the complex and demanding environment of the classroom.

We have been fortunate enough to have the support of our school system in bringing about change. Change begins with the individual, however, and each individual teacher can make a difference. We believe that the integration of technology into every classroom is essential and that it will excite and enhance learning of students and teachers alike.

Some of the greatest gifts a teacher can give today's students are the ability to cope with change; an understanding of the necessity to be risk-takers, problem solvers, and lifelong learners; and the skills to be successful in a complicated technological world.

Introduction

A hum of activity fills the room. In the corner, students are gathered around the TV, engrossed in a video about alternative energy sources. Two partners are using a video camera to produce a news broadcast about a local issue. Intent on their project, they pay no attention to their friends nearby who are researching the causes of an environmental problem, using an encyclopedia stored on CD-ROM. At a bank of computers against the wall, pairs of students are obviously deeply involved in their tasks. A closer look reveals that each team is doing something different: setting up a simulated island ecosystem, using a graphics program to design an energy-efficient transportation system, writing a poem about the environment, building a database of endangered species, learning to spell vocabulary related to the environmental theme, communicating via modem with a classmate who is hospitalized, and using a telecommunications network to interview a scientist at a remote research station in the Arctic. It's hard to find the teacher at first, but there she is, working with a small group of students who are listening to a story on tape as they read along in their books. Once they are settled, she moves on to check the progress of two other students, who are building a water filter at the back of the classroom.

This scenario is what you might see if you peeked into a technological classroom in action, but this brief glance probably raises more questions than it answers. What is a technological classroom? Why is it important? Do you have such a classroom? Can you create one? What do you need? How is it done?

This book is designed to answer those questions. In it, we examine the theoretical and practical issues surrounding the technological classroom. It is based on our experience in designing and implementing technology-integrated curriculum. The ideas evolved over a period of five years and have been successfully used by more than a hundred teachers and thousands of students. Our initial technological classrooms, developed for 9- to 12-year-old students, have since become a model for more senior classes also.

A number of assumptions underlie the philosophy we present in this book:

- Technology should be viewed as a tool to assist in the acquisition of knowledge and development of skills rather than as an end in itself.
- Technology can improve student learning, particularly in the areas of accessing information and problem solving, and can assist in preparing students for the labor force.
- Each kind of technology has specific strengths that need to be recognized and maximized.
- The use of technology must be integrated into the curriculum and day-to-day experiences of the student.
- For significant change to occur and continue, the educator should understand the change process and be provided with ongoing support throughout the process of integrating technology into students' daily school experiences.

Whenever we as teachers undertake a change in curriculum delivery, in teaching methods and styles, it is not a decision to be taken lightly. Being aware that the progress of our students is at stake, we can be reluctant to proceed until all of our questions are answered. We feel the need to be sure that the transition will be smooth and that every student will benefit. So it is that this book addresses the many practical issues that accompany the introduction of technology into the classroom. Our goal is to include topics about which we are most frequently asked:

- How do I get started?
- From whom can I learn?
- Where do I go for help?
- What equipment do I need?
- How do I learn to use the hardware and software?
- Where can the money for equipment be obtained?
- Where will I put this equipment?
- How can I arrange my classroom to facilitate student use of the technology?
- Are there safety factors that I should consider?
- How do I set up and control workstations?
- How do I teach students to use the hardware and software?
- How can I ensure that my students care for the equipment properly?
- How can technology make my classroom more student-centered?
- How can technology help me to individualize my program?
- Where do mastery learning and cooperative learning fit in?
- What methods can my students use to keep track of completed activities?
- What kinds of record-keeping are most appropriate for teachers?
- What about evaluation in this setting?
- What should I say to parents?
- In what ways can technology assist students with special needs?
- Should I change the way in which my timetable is organized?
- How can I arrange equal accessibility to the technology for all students in my class?
- What is the role of the teacher in this environment?

- In what ways can technology make me more efficient in my job?
- How can I get others involved?
- How will I cope with this change?

Because we believe that good classroom practices derive from carefully researched theories, we provide practical strategies based on both research and experience. We hope you will use the ideas in this book to develop your own philosophy and personal approach to integrating technology into your day-to-day teaching strategies.

We cannot provide a resource to suit the needs of all grades in all subject areas, but we can provide a sample of possibilities based on what has worked for us and others. The practical suggestions are intended to be motivators and thought-provoking starting points that you can adapt and modify to suit your own situation, your needs, and your students' needs.

Whether you are new to technology, simply interested in change, or reconsidering the present use of technology in your classroom, we hope that the results of our research and experience, as presented in this book, are helpful and will enable you to work more effectively. Above all else, we hope that the addition of technology to your classroom will be an exciting and enriching experience for you and your students!

■ [In a technology-rich classroom] students completed their assignments with greater enthusiasm and success because of the greater variety of auditory, visual, and kinesthetic experiences. (Alana Morris and Sandra Tischer, teachers)

CHAPTER 1

Why Integrate Technology into the Classroom?

Technology can be used to enhance instruction and expand the limits of the existing curriculum. As an information tool, it can be used to obtain, organize, manipulate and communicate knowledge and information. It can help to address the range of differing learning styles and the different modalities of individual learning strengths. By tapping into its power, students can expand their access to the world around them.[1]

What is the technological classroom? It is more than simply the use of computer hardware and software within a traditional environment. The technological classroom is a setting that uses technologies such as interactive videotape and videodisc, computer-assisted learning, electronic access to information, distance learning, audiovisual aids, and hypermedia to create a superior learning environment for teachers and students. It is information-rich, student-centered, and active. It is a classroom in which the variety of technology helps students to acquire academic, technological, and social skills. In the technological classroom, technologies are integrated with the best pedagogy of the time, in order to empower students and teachers to move toward a new vision of education.

Why is technology in education important? What can we learn from research and past experience? What lies ahead? This first chapter will help you to develop a personal rationale for the integration of technology into the school curriculum. We believe that there are important reasons for adopting the new model of the technology-enhanced classroom:

- Our students live in a world of technology.
- New technologies can enrich and expand learning, increase the productivity of teachers and students, and enhance their lives beyond the classroom.
- There is an ever-widening diversity of student needs in every classroom and these students have different learning preferences.
- The workplace demands a new repertoire of skills and competencies.

Schools should reflect the real world in which their students live. Today, the computer-literate can do their banking, monitor the stock market, order an airline ticket, telecommunicate with people in other countries, and listen to a recording of Beethoven.

Our changing world

Technology is transforming our world. This technological revolution is changing the way we learn, the way we work, and the way we live. Technology is at the heart of global communications networks, advances in medical science, the "smart house," computer animation, musical composition, weather forecasting, and so much more of our lives. The day-to-day experiences of today's students are not like those of yesterday's.

 Today's students live in a technological environment. Learning about the highly technological environment in which we live is critical to today's students. They will need to function well in it and make intelligent decisions about the relationships among humans, technology, and the natural environment. In our society, power is held and will continue to be held by those who have developed the important skills of obtaining, evaluating, and generating information. Parents and society expect educational institutions to prepare students for the world in which they will live. Students of today will be the adults of the 21st century. Although we cannot be certain about the exact nature of their adult world, we can predict that technology will continue to play an important role. Our students already live in a world of technology; our education system must now change to adequately prepare them for this reality.

> ■ We have gone through three waves of technological change. . . . The first wave was when we used tools to do work. . . . The second wave was when we began to have the technology to do some of those tasks, the manual application of technology. . . . The third wave is when we have the technology do the task.[2]

Enriched learning and increased productivity

In years past, students had the inkwell, the pen, and one book at a time. They were expected to learn disciplined control over a fragmented world. They were not taught analysis, synthesis, evaluation, or integration of tasks. Knowledge was taught as an end in itself and not as a means to more general skills such as problem solving.[3] In the classroom of the past, learning meant memorization demonstrated by performance on tests.

Today, new technologies help teachers to respond to the different learning styles of students and to develop new attitudes toward learning. Technology helps students to become better problem solvers, increases their motivation, and allows students to take more responsibility for their own learning. We want our students to learn how to acquire information and to develop both cognitive and communication skills. Information technologies can access information quickly, assist in the analysis and organization of data, and provide the ability to communicate with others.

When computers were first introduced into the classroom they were used primarily for drill and practice. Teachers frequently used computer access as a reward. Now, computers have numerous applications, from word processing to interactivity. Research is filled with impressive statistics about the use of computers in education, as the following examples illustrate:

- One computerized instruction program was shown to help students master basic skills in reading, writing, and mathematics and also boosted attendance and self-esteem.[4]
- The impact of computers on children's self-esteem and self-confidence is substantiated in other studies.[5]
- Computer-aided learning has been shown to improve general attitudes toward school.[6]
- Computer-aided instruction has also been shown to improve mathematics scores.[7]
- In research conducted in the Apple Classrooms of Tomorrow (ACOT), Robert Tierney[8] discovered that where computer use was integrated into students' daily experiences, the students developed a sense of purpose and saw the connection between their work and the world around them. Students were self-confident about their computer skills, were more inclined to review their ideas and written work, and were more willing to share with others. The computer was seen as providing the opportunity to enhance student thinking skills and develop problem-solving skills.

The motivational appeal of working with technology adds to both skill development and positive attitudes toward learning. Technology can increase the productivity of teachers and students through the effective use of word processing and publishing tools, electronic and voice mail, authoring systems to create learning materials, and access to information through telecommunications and information storage such as CD-ROM databases. Computers and the great variety of technology available today have the potential to change education as we know it.

> ■ I guess the best way to describe how the kids view the [technology-integrated] program is when I tell them that we are starting a new unit, they all cheer. That speaks for itself. (Sandra Tischer, teacher)

The learner

We have a great diversity of students in our classrooms today, each with specific needs to be met. The uniqueness of students is reflected in their different styles of learning. These styles, or modalities, are the channels through which individuals receive and remember information. The three educationally relevant channels are the visual, auditory, and kinesthetic. Teaching to modality strengths can be a powerful tool. Students with a visual preference benefit from the delivery of skills through such media as videotapes, videodiscs, and computer programs that use colorful graphics or animation. Others who learn best through auditory channels benefit from technologies that use sound to enhance what is on the screen. For kinesthetic learners, robotics and computer-controlled devices enhance the manipulation of materials and make learning meaningful. Multimedia technologies are multisensory; thus, they combine several modes of learning. Technology enables you to provide a variety of teaching and learning strategies that address the learning preferences of students. The issue is ". . . not to identify the 'best' medium but to vary instructional methods and technologies meaningfully and effectively."[9]

■ Some of the most interesting work in learning today is occurring at MIT's Center for Arts and Media. The Center's experiments with mixed media, combining text windows, full-motion TV-quality video windows, and speech as part of interactive learning tools, have astonished researchers. Children, contrary to what their parents believe, can listen to U-2 on the radio and watch "Miami Vice" on television with an open book on the floor, doing their mathematics homework. Rather than being distracted by the bombardment of media, they find that the "mixed messages" have the potential to help them learn. If individuals can simultaneously get relevant information in a choice of media, they will become far more effective learners. This is exactly where personal computing is headed in the 1990s.[10]

Because it is unlikely that you will have a computer or other specific technology for every student in your class, the integration of technology in the classroom leads naturally to a variety of teaching styles. Research indicates many positive aspects of different methods of instruction. Several studies have compared the effects of whole-class instruction with more student-centered environments. Whole-class instruction has been found to be slightly more effective in learning basic skills such as reading, writing, spelling, and arithmetic, while students in more open classrooms develop more positive attitudes toward school and more creativity, independence, curiosity, and cooperation.[11]

However, the use of activity-based learning also has benefits for skill development. It has elevated achievement scores in science and mathematics.[12] Cooperative learning was found to enhance mathematical achievement,[13] as well as improving affective and cognitive development.[14] The best strategy seems to be to alternate or combine teaching/learning styles. By combining individualized instruction with cooperative learning, improvement was seen in students' reading and writing achievement, vocabulary, language expression, and reading proficiency.[15] Terwell[16] found that greater variety in teaching strategies in mathematics programs for students aged 12 to 16 led to greater improvement in mathematics achievement. This research adds new meaning to the old saying "Variety is the spice of life."

The workplace

■ To rekindle old debates about dropping the standards of the past misses the point. Educators debated the demise of writing when the fountain pen was replaced by the ball-point pen and the loss of mathematical skills when electronic calculators appeared. The world will not linger in the past in matters of employment skills. We must prepare our students to work in *their* future not in *our* past.[17]

Many of today's students will enter the working world in the next century. As well as reading, writing, and computational skills, the workplace demands technological competence. The technology and skills being used in most of today's schools are already many years behind those in the existing workplace. In some cases, education is so far out of step with the workplace that students may actually have to unlearn what the schools are teaching when they enter the work force. We must face the fact that technological illiterates will be unable to compete in a global economy in which technological skills are required. "If computers are not successfully and widely integrated into primary and secondary education our society will stratify into those with the knowledge to succeed and those who cannot."[18] The question is no longer *should* education change but rather, how can it keep pace with the change that is occurring in the workplace. The challenge is to change carefully and thoughtfully, yet at a pace to accommodate workplace needs.

■ Bob Hughes, Boeing's corporate director of education relations, looks to computer networks as a key to turning out students who adapt regularly to change and who solve problems by seeking out and applying new ideas. The traditional classroom, he says, is singularly ill suited to producing lifelong learners: "Right now, you've got 30 little workers who come into a room, sit in rows, follow instructions from a boss, and can't talk to one another. School is the last time they'll ever see that model."[19]

The change in the workplace is more than just technological. Today's employers are looking for a high-quality work force with specific skills, attitudes, and behaviors. Organizations of old were largely characterized by specialists performing specific tasks. Employees' tasks were organized by supervisors and the valued employee was one who would follow instructions and perform rote tasks. In most cases, administration was responsible for thinking, motivation, implementation, and discipline.

The needs of today's organization are very different. Future-oriented businesses are looking for workers who are flexible and who possess problem-solving abilities as well as excellent communication skills. The ability to work as a team member is essential in this style of organization. With the increase in both the amount of information and its rapid dissemination, learning must be a lifelong experience for everyone and workers will need to upgrade their skills regularly.

■ Gholson of IBM made the following predictions in 1990:

- 80% of the jobs required in the year 2000 do not exist at this time.
- 70% of these new jobs will require two years of education beyond high school and 35% will require four years of post-secondary education.
- Most jobs presently held by school dropouts will be done by robots in the year 2000.
- Lifelong learning will become a reality. For example, an engineer's specialized knowledge is already replaced by more current information in 3.2 years.[20]

In a study conducted by the Canadian Corporate Council on Education,[21] employers in both large and small businesses stated that they were looking for academic skills, personal management skills, and teamwork skills. The resulting *Employability Skills Profile* described each of these areas.

Academic skills include:

- communication skills (speaking, listening, reading, and writing);
- thinking skills (the ability to think logically and critically, to solve problems, to use technology and information systems effectively and to access and apply specialized knowledge);
- learning skills with a view of learning as a lifelong process.

Personal management skills include:

- positive attitude and behavior based on self-confidence and high personal standards;
- a sense of responsibility, including time management, setting goals, and accountability;
- adaptability.

Teamwork skills are seen by the Canadian Corporate Council on Education to be equally important. The ability to work with others, to respect their opinions, and to exercise cooperation are just a few of these necessary skills. We believe that an active, student-centered, technological classroom facilitates the learning of these important skills.

Why is business so interested in the nature of education? Profit and the nation's commercial advantage are strongly linked to how well the education system manages technology and innovation. Students who are exposed to technology in school will have a definite advantage when entering the workplace.[22]

■ Lately in the newspaper you read that you have to be able to use a computer to get a good job. . . . Having the experience now will help you when you are older. (Student)

Past experience

The success record of innovations in education is not encouraging; in fact, the way teachers teach has changed little since the days of the one-room schoolhouse. We tend to teach as we were taught. Teachers still spend a significant part of each day lecturing and students are still viewed as one group rather than as individuals requiring individual programs. Emphasis is still often on rote learning, following instructions, and performing routine tasks. Is it any wonder that many countries have literacy concerns and are puzzled over high dropout rates?

> ■ Indeed, facility in using a computer has become one of the marks of an educated person. The "disadvantaged" student of the 1990s will be the one who is afraid, inexperienced or ignorant of computers. And so it is alarming that our public schools in general have not done well in integrating computers into their curricula.[23]

Consider for a moment a few innovations that were viewed to have great potential but have since lost their impact: radio, television, and computer-assisted learning. For a brief period, educators were presented with the numerous ways that these technologies could be used in the classroom. When the emphasis was shifted to the next innovation, the previous one appears to have been forgotten. Technology was frequently an extra rather than an integral part of the student's day-to-day experiences. The skeptic might believe that, since previous attempts to integrate technology have not met with success, present-day innovations will meet the same fate. The interactive nature of today's technologies, however, makes them different. Because of the ways in which they can be used, they have the power to revolutionize education and forever alter the roles of teachers and students.

The single greatest obstacle to the incorporation of technology into the students' daily life is money. In business, the acquisition of technology is viewed as an investment, as opposed to a cost. In the same way, schools must learn to see technology as an essential classroom component, as important as pencils, paper, and books. Restructuring of budgets and reallocation of funds may be required to accomplish this. For example, some of the money now used to photocopy worksheets could be used for CD-ROM resources or a modem, telephone line, and access to a telecommunications system. When government funding does not allow educational systems to turn their priorities into realities, then schools may investigate other avenues, such as business/education partnerships. In Chapter 2, business/education relationships are discussed in greater detail.

Another problem associated with the full use of technology in the classroom has been the absence of its integration into existing curricula. Technology has been viewed as either an add-on to the existing curriculum or as a subject in itself. This leads to an incorrect view, by students, of the role of technology in school life: that of a special event or an optional subject for *some* students. The technological classroom provides a solution.

> ■ There is a difference between what is happening in education and what is happening in other work settings. The difference is that while other institutions and work settings have adopted the technologies into the heart of their functioning, and the technologies, in turn, have changed the nature of the work, education has not changed a single basic process that is essential to its operation. Education has tended to keep the technologies apart from the basic processes of learning and teaching.[24]

Future trends

D.P. Ely, in an article "Trends and Issues in Educational Technology," [25] identifies some trends that have already appeared in technology use in education; among them:

- concern for design and development of good instructional products and procedures;
- evaluation as an important part of the design and development of instructional products;
- research and development knowledge being used to solve teaching and learning problems;
- computers found in nearly every U.S. public school;
- interactive video accepted as an important research and development tool but not yet accepted in schools and higher education;
- distance learning regarded as a major vehicle for instruction at all levels;
- impact of technology on individuals examined through research;
- applications of telecommunications used in society reflected in schools.

These kinds of observations cast a positive light on the progress already being made in the use of technology in education. New technology is also an important factor influencing changes in the nature of education.

Figure 1.1

Some changes in education

Element	Old Views	New Trends
Teacher's role	Conveyer of information Interpreter of information	Coach and guide
Nature of student	Recipient of information A vessel to be filled	Self-motivated learner Problem solver Individualized learner
Resources	Sets of textbooks used in a linear fashion Teacher-selected materials	Variety of print and non-print resources Students select materials from a variety provided by the teacher
Curriculum	Emphasis on content Divided into distinct subject areas	Emphasis on skills Holistic, integrated curriculum
Evaluation	Tests and examinations Content-based evaluation	Variety of techniques - tests, conferences, peer evaluation, self-evaluation Quality of performance Emphasis on daily work
Community	Delegates responsibility to educators	Involved in decisions Provides input into curriculum

■ There are more hours of pedagogy in one thirty-second [television] commercial than most teachers can pack into a month of teaching. The subject matter of the TV commercial is quite secondary; what matters is the skill, professionalism, and persuasive power of the presentation. Children therefore come to school today with expectations that are bound to be disappointed and frustrated. . . . Schools will increasingly be forced to use computers, television, films, videotapes, and audiotapes. The teacher increasingly will become a supervisor and a mentor — very much, perhaps, the way he functioned in the medieval university some hundreds of years ago. The teacher's job will be to help, to lead, to set examples, to encourage; it may not primarily be to convey the subject matter itself.[26]

CHAPTER 2

Where Are You Going?

Nothing is more important in our society, by definition, than the education of our youth. Nothing in pursuit of educational excellence is more important than studying the models of things that work.[1]

B efore starting on a journey, you decide where you are going. For a technological journey you need to do the same. What are your goals for the integration of technology in your school or classroom? We suggest the following:

- to enable learners to use technology to acquire the knowledge, skills, and attitudes they will need;
- to provide opportunities for learners to use technology for a wide variety of purposes (e.g., accessing information, organizing data, exploring, creating, problem solving);
- to incorporate the use of technology into all areas of the curriculum at all levels;
- to encourage learners to use technology naturally as an everyday part of the learning process;
- to involve learners in using technology on an equitable basis;
- to help learners think critically about technology in order to use it effectively and appropriately;
- to enhance teacher productivity by using technology as a tool.

While we were struggling to define a model of technology integration that would complement these goals, we saw many different prototypes in action. They varied from the million-dollar facility to a classroom with one computer in the corner. You may be starting from scratch with your own vision or working within the boundaries of an established plan. You may have only a limited effect on the vision toward which your school or school system aspires but you may have opportunities to influence decisions. It is better to help shape the future than to have it imposed on you. When you finish reading this chapter, you will have an idea of the variety of potential ways in which you can integrate technology. The technological classroom is the most viable and effective way of achieving the goals outlined above.

The technological classroom is not a classroom for the future but a classroom for today. The comments from teachers and students that you will read throughout this book are testimony to the fact that it is a necessary and exciting change. Change is never easy, so in this chapter, we look briefly at the change process in both theory and practice.

You need not feel you are facing the challenge of technology alone. Partnerships with the business community can be of great assistance in achieving your goal of integrating technology into the daily life of students. We offer some practical considerations for establishing and maintaining such partnerships.

The Cadillac version: The technological school

Most people imagine the technological school not as the school of today, but as the school of the new millennium. In fact, these schools already exist today in a number of locations around the world. They are generally made possible through corporate partnerships, special grants from the business community, and the dedication of small groups of enlightened educators. Envision a school in which all computing resources are networked and integrated to make information sources available to everyone who needs them. The communications network includes electronic mail, bulletin boards, electronic conferencing, and access to global telecommunications. Information is processed through the use of word processing applications, databases, spreadsheets,

Figure 2.1

This school of the future is here today.

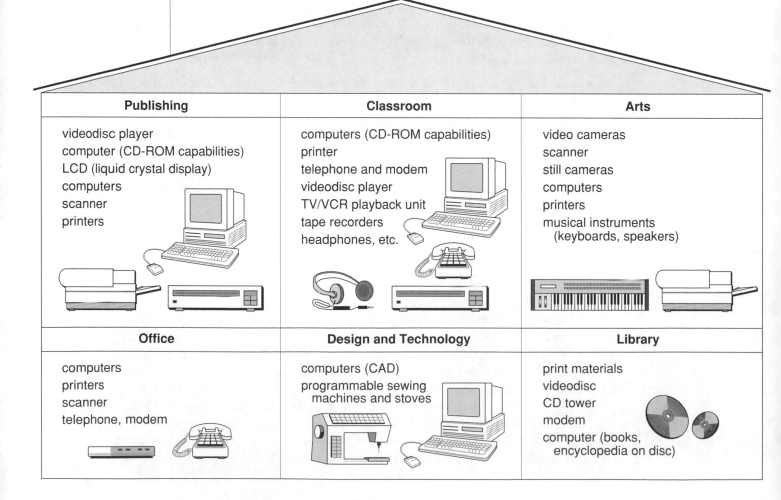

Publishing	Classroom	Arts
videodisc player computer (CD-ROM capabilities) LCD (liquid crystal display) computers scanner printers	computers (CD-ROM capabilities) printer telephone and modem videodisc player TV/VCR playback unit tape recorders headphones, etc.	video cameras scanner still cameras computers printers musical instruments (keyboards, speakers)
Office	**Design and Technology**	**Library**
computers printers scanner telephone, modem	computers (CAD) programmable sewing machines and stoves	print materials videodisc CD tower modem computer (books, encyclopedia on disc)

and desktop publishing. Although each student may not have a personal computer, they are abundant enough that access is seldom, if ever, a problem. Teachers and students have curricula that fully integrate technology, multimedia products for teaching and individualized learning, test-item banks, and learning management systems that track and record student progress. In the school library, electronic resources are available for a wide range of topics and the on-line catalog can be accessed from any classroom location.

The standard sedan version: The technological classroom

The reality in many schools and school systems is that we are dealing with old buildings, limited funds for the purchase and maintenance of equipment, and a traditional curriculum. Despite these limitations, it is possible to establish very workable technology-integrated classrooms.

The process begins with leaders who have vision and who consider the integration of technology to be of the highest priority. It can be successful only through the efforts of committed, hard-working teachers who are willing and eager to change. You may find that, because technology allows you to optimize resources, you can reallocate funds to technology from other areas of the budget. By setting up some basic equipment and developing a curriculum that assists in its integrated use in daily activities, you can create a technological learning environment.

We will explore this "standard sedan" model in great depth, but to give you an idea of how much equipment you might require, we recommend the following:

- 3 to 5 computers, one of which has CD-ROM capabilities
- a printer
- a telephone
- a modem
- a videodisc player
- a TV/VCR playback unit
- 2 or 3 tape recorders
- headphones
- power bars
- assorted storage containers

Put these in your classroom, apply them in a variety of ways, and things can change! Natural use of technology as a tool can develop in this setting. You have the flexibility to organize a total learning environment that reflects the integration of the technology. The resources are available whenever students require them. You are not limited to specific subjects or time frames. In the chapters ahead, we will look at the many ways in which these tools can be integrated into the curriculum to improve and enhance student learning.

■ We believe . . . that the eventual long-term success of computer education depends on widespread use of computers as teaching and learning tools in individual classrooms.[2]

When each classroom has its own computers, a school computer lab takes on a new role. Rather than being a room where students go to "do" computer for a period of time, it is used for introducing new software, for direct instruction, for testing purposes, and for allowing greater access to students as they explore and try out new software.

> ■ It [the technology-integrated classroom] gives me the chance to see my kids as individuals and to work with them as individuals. I have 27 individuals and I can see 27 kids growing in leaps and bounds in every different direction because of the technology. It's not new to them: it's part of their education. It's part of their learning. (Jim Rogers, teacher)

The super-economy model: The one-computer classroom

We have seen teachers with access to only one computer discouraged by what they feel to be a situation with little potential. However, we have also seen what determination, creativity, and adaptability can accomplish. One computer can serve a lot of students if you keep it going at all times, making sure that all students are scheduled equitably to use it. For any unit that you teach, you will be able to turn up at least one piece of software that can be incorporated into that unit. You can use your computer as a teaching tool for large-group instruction, as a workstation for an individual or small group, and as a personal secretary and record-keeper for you and your students. You can round up simple technologies such as filmstrip viewers and tape recorders.

Remember, one of the greatest skills you can teach your students is fearless curiosity — the willingness to explore and learn about *any* technology. By working with the technology you have, you demonstrate that you are comfortable with technology, that you view it as important, and that you are ready and willing to move ahead when the opportunity arises. Many of the practical ideas we offer can be adapted for use in the one-computer classroom.

> ■ A computer can be used in a variety of ways in the one-computer classroom:
> - one computer and large groups
> - one computer and small groups
> - one computer as a lecture tool
> - one computer as a learning center
> - one computer as your secretary[3]

Other strategies

Because the integration of technology can appear to be an expensive venture, we see schools experimenting with different adaptations of the technological classroom in their search for a cost-effective method. The variables of each situation are too numerous to mention, but you might consider the following options.

Shared classrooms

One cost-effective idea is for two classes of students to share one set of equipment. Initially this seems like a good idea, given that there is a portion of the school day in which the equipment would be underutilized (e.g., during physical education, vocal music, or drama classes). It facilitates maximum use of the technology, encourages teachers to plan and work as a team, and increases student interaction between classes.

Schools that have tried this option, however, have experienced some disadvantages:

- The movement of students from room to room wastes valuable time and causes innumerable small problems with managing both students' and teachers' materials and possessions.
- Nobody takes ownership and responsibility for the care, storage, and maintenance of equipment.
- Personality differences and different styles, standards, and expectations of the teachers involved can lead to an unpleasant working relationship.

School technology room

Another possibility is a special multimedia or technology room within the school to which all classes have access on a rotational basis. This room can be equipped with the latest in technology. Imagine a three-dimensional scanner, video cameras with playback units, videodisc players, a modem and computer for telecommunications, several CD-ROM units with a selection of materials to be used on them, multimedia software with assorted peripherals, and desktop publishing materials of all kinds! A site administrator can be assigned the responsibility of helping teachers and students, organizing the work space, and caring for the equipment. At first thought, this might appear very attractive, but it also has some serious drawbacks:

- Technology cannot be viewed as a tool to accomplish many specific tasks, because it is not available whenever the student needs it.
- The teacher cannot naturally integrate technology into the daily experience of each student. It becomes a special event.
- The teacher does not have easy access to the technology for previewing resources or for personal use.
- Neither student nor teacher learns to take responsibility for the care and appropriate use of the equipment.
- Time-lines for the use of the room are artificial, arbitrary, and determined by administrative needs rather than by student needs.

However, any teacher would undoubtedly be happy to see the establishment of a school technology center *in addition to* technological classrooms, to be used for more specialized applications.

> ■ When computers are kept in special rooms, taught by special teachers for special students, the message is that computers are not for everyone. Who will shy away first? The kids, who know who those special people are and that they themselves aren't among them.[4]

High-tech center

Some school systems extend the concept of the technological classroom to an even broader context by creating a high-tech center that serves several schools in a district. This allows for the availability of the latest and greatest technology and the specialists to operate it. Unfortunately, it magnifies all of the disadvantages of the school technology center, as well as adding transportation costs.

None of these alternatives, however, serve students as well as when they have access to technology in their own classroom, even if this is less sophisticated technology.

Making the journey

When you take the first steps to make technology an integral part of the teaching/ learning process, you begin a journey that will change you as a professional and will change your students' perspective and experience of school. Creating a technological classroom will require you to change your ideas about how teachers teach and how students learn. It is important to know that the transformation in your classroom will be ongoing and that every day might not be the success you hoped it would be. Educational experts in implementation and the change process[5] state that:

- Change takes place over time.
- Change is a process.
- Change involves anxiety.
- Technical assistance and psychological support are crucial.
- Change involves learning new skills through practice.
- Successful change involves pressure.
- The people who implement the changes need to see why the new way works better.

We can try to turn back from change whenever the going gets tough or we can learn to embrace it, viewing challenges as opportunities. It is these very opportunities that for many rekindle that excitement they felt on the first day of their teaching career.

Change brings with it a series of challenges. Your responses determine the effectiveness of the change.

The nature of the change will determine to what extent the change is implemented.[6] Some factors that may affect the implementation of technology into the classroom include:

- the complexity of the change: In addition to adding technology to my classroom, will it change my teaching role?

- its explicitness: Are there specific measurable outcomes?

- its practicability: Is there space for the new equipment?

- its adaptability: Can it be used by teachers and students?

- its communicability: Will I be able to clearly explain to administrators and parents how I am incorporating technology?

The innovation we describe in this book involves more than just the addition of technology to an existing classroom environment. It requires learning new technologies, restructuring the roles of teacher and student, developing strategies for cooperative and individualized learning, timetabling, and organizational changes. Therefore, as an innovation, it is indeed complex and demands a significant amount of change.

A project's outcome depends to a great extent on the setting — elements such as the school's leadership, staff and staff-student relationships, and the physical environment. An orderly, secure, and supportive environment will make the introduction of a new way of teaching easier.

Figure 2.2

Knowledge of stages of change will help to guide you through the process. This model is based on the work of many change theorists.[7] Stages of change are described in greater detail in Appendix 1.

If you are pursuing the integration of technology as a personal initiative, you are responsible for convincing all of the stakeholders of the validity of the change, obtaining funding, and pursuing the necessary expertise. Discuss with your principal exactly what you are planning to do and be ready to support your plans with the results of research as well as of your own practical classroom experience. The school principal is critical to the ongoing success of your innovation, and in the days ahead you may require monetary, philosophical, and/or pedagogical support. On the other hand, if your initiative is supported at the school and/or system level, you will find the change much easier and support from both peers and experts will be available when you need it.

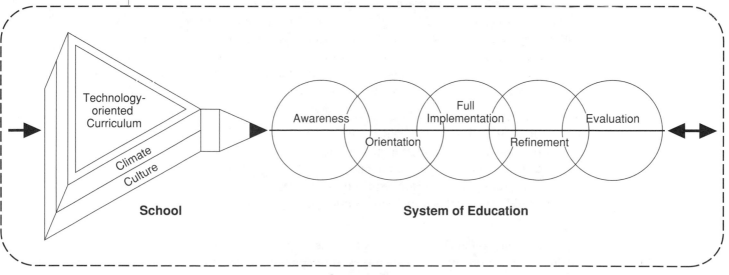

"Culture" is the shared beliefs or values that guide behavior. "Climate" is the personality or work environment of the school.

Business partnerships

As you embark on your journey, explore the possibilities of establishing a partnership with a business. A true business/education partnership includes the recognition by *both* parties of a shared problem, shared resources, and a balance of beneficial outcomes. Concerns such as an unstable economy, high energy costs, and declining productivity are common to both business and education.[8] When a business and a school make a commitment to a mutually beneficial venture, a partnership is established. Technology often serves as the meeting ground for business/education partnerships, because both rely on technology to accomplish their goals and because technology-based projects can be specific and achievable.

■ Through partnerships, businesses can dramatically influence the quality of education for students — and the skills those students eventually bring to a career. Businesses do this by supporting:

- innovative science, math, and technology projects, both inside and outside the classroom;
- scholarships, guaranteed jobs, and school tuition costs for students who meet certain standards for academic achievement, and who otherwise would never reach college;
- mentor/tutor programs that make it possible for blue-collar and white-collar employees to tutor individual students;
- development of curriculum materials on workplace literacy that give students the skills and knowledge they need as future employees;
- technology acquisition — such as computers, lab equipment, and telecommunications equipment — that helps students learn a variety of skills at their own interest level and pace.[9]

For a school, the advantages of establishing a partnership with one or more businesses include the opportunity to obtain leadership and advice from experts; financial assistance in the form of grants, gifts, or equipment; opportunities for student internship and career awareness; the provision of support services in hardware and/or software; and perhaps a higher profile for the school in the community that it serves. From the perspective of a business corporation, for what reasons would a company enter into a partnership with an educational institution? The reasons might include:

- public relations and media exposure;
- immediate or long-term financial gains;
- brand-name recognition at an early age;
- testing ground for new products;
- opportunity to learn from educator expertise;
- need for graduates trained in high-technology areas;
- altruism.

The shareholders of a company are generally more interested in increasing the value of the company's stock than they are in public relations. If their product can be showcased in the school or if its use in the school leads to an increase in sales, then the company would obviously be more interested in becoming involved in a joint venture. When considering a business partnership, keep in mind the importance of dialogue — a better understanding from both sides. For example, how many people in business realize that a professional teacher does not usually even have a telephone? On the other hand, a partnership with business will underline for teachers how important their work is in preparing students for the work force. Tolbert[10] suggests the following guidelines to establishing a good relationship between business and education:

- Understand the unique roles, needs, and expectations of each party.
- Understand the responsibilities of each partner.
- Formalize an agreement between institutions not individuals.
- Use peer review and/or endorsement by outside experts.

Finding a business partnership

Finding a corporate partner with which to join forces may not be easy. As educators, most of us possess neither the skills nor the strategies we need to approach the wider community for support. We may feel naive and in danger of being victimized by business marketing skills. How do you go about it? There is no guaranteed recipe for success, but here are some hints that we have found to be helpful:

- Identify companies within your district and companies whose products you are already using. These will have the greatest potential for an interest in any new venture you undertake.
- Explore personal contacts such as parents of students in your school.
- Consider public service agencies, civic organizations, local government agencies, and cultural and special-interest groups.
- Find out as much as possible about potential partners and their needs.
- Show people from the business community that you are taking the first steps by yourself, rather than waiting for a savior to come along. Open the doors of your school and show them the great things that are already starting to happen through technology.
- Generate as much publicity for your new ventures in technology as you can. Try to establish your school as an innovative leader. Everyone likes a winner.
- Be prepared to be specific about what a corporate sponsor could do for your school or project and what they would receive in return.

Keep in mind that the most beneficial partnership for both parties is accomplished through long-term planning and cooperation, rather than through an isolated donation or a special project. By keeping the communication lines open, setting clearly defined and measurable goals, ensuring the accountability of both partners, and problem solving together, you can enhance the success of your partnership.

CHAPTER 3

What About Equipment?

A 1985 report from the Southeastern Educational Improvement Laboratory suggests that schools and contemporary teaching styles are creations of, and remain captive to, print technology. The report highlights the great gap that exists between print-oriented teachers on the one hand and technology-oriented students on the other, who reflect the pace and style of the technologies that dominate their lives. As long as education continues to be immersed in print technologies constructs about the world, the report states, there will continue to be a great gap between the way teachers teach and the way students learn.[1]

Every technological classroom is equipped somewhat differently. In Chapter 2, "Where Are You Going?" we listed some equipment requirements that are basic in the establishment of a technological classroom. Certainly, the success of your technological classroom depends much more on how you use the equipment than on what equipment you have, but some of the most difficult decisions *do* revolve around selecting, purchasing, and maintaining hardware.

It is not our intention in this book to rate or promote various brands of hardware. Instead, this chapter will provide you with a successful model for long-term planning, general guidelines for selecting and maintaining hardware, specific considerations about certain types of equipment, and practical tips about warranties and servicing of equipment.

Planning for equipment purchase and maintenance

Much of the technological equipment that has been purchased for schools remains dust-covered due to lack of use. Why has this occurred? One of the main reasons is lack of planning, before acquisition, for its maintenance and use. Without a plan, it is easy to lose sight of your goals. A technology plan also addresses many issues other than the purchase and maintenance of equipment (e.g., procedures for evaluating software, equitable access, technology-related teacher training, evaluation procedures). We provide complete guidelines for writing a technology plan in Appendix 2, page 151.

The number of choices available, especially in computer hardware, is enough to overwhelm even the most technology-literate person! The appeal of the latest state-of-the-art developments and leading-edge technologies can distract you from their actual use and cost-effectiveness in educating students. Selection of hardware involves a variety of important factors:

- inventory of current hardware;
- goals for the use of hardware;
- current and future hardware needs;
- compatibility with other equipment;
- supplier;
- price;
- uses by students and teachers;
- training required for students and teachers;
- amount of use;

- durability;
- ease of upgrading (if required);
- ease and cost of repair;
- availability of parts;
- warranty;
- electrical requirements;
- safety;
- security;
- furniture required.

Create a consultation process that will address all planning requirements. The purchasing officer for the school system, if there is one, can provide a wealth of information about possible suppliers and costs. Most distributors are delighted to be invited to demonstrate their products. The latest technology, however, may not always be the best for your classroom or school, so be sure that salespeople are well briefed and have a clear understanding of your needs before they make proposals. A technical expert can provide maintenance and repair advice. You might find a person in the community, perhaps a parent, who is knowledgeable and prepared to act as a technical adviser. If your school system does not have a hardware technician, perhaps now is the time to plan to hire someone.

■ Putting educational goals first also applies when selecting multimedia equipment vendors, notes Eliot Levinson, a senior consultant for Pelavin Associates, Inc., who helps school districts set up technology management organizations. Rather than letting vendors "hustle schools . . . telling them that if they take [the vendor's] system, they can get anything out of it they want," Levinson advises school leaders to ask the right questions and set up specifications for vendors to meet. "For example," says Levinson, "lay out five problems that you would like solved, and give the list to the vendors. Let them demonstrate that they can help you solve your specific problems."[2]

A broad view of the potential management and use of the equipment by staff and students can be provided by the school principal. A superintendent or supervisory officer can articulate the vision and overall goals of the school system. The involvement of staff members representing various levels and curriculum areas is critical, because they are in touch with the realities of using technology in their unique teaching situations. These teachers can also provide a testing environment for trying out various products: field-testing potential purchases before investing can save time and money and avoid later frustration. The planning team should also include representatives from community stakeholders such as parents and businesspeople, as this may be an appropriate opportunity to underline wider involvement in your school.

Figure 3.1

When the decision-making team consults with all individuals who will be affected by a purchase, it ensures that many different perspectives are considered.

Input for the Decision-making Team

Trustees/Elected Officials	• What are the educational outcomes? • What is the associated cost?
Supervisory Officer	• What is the effect on teacher(s) and students at the system level and the classroom level? • What are the budgetary implications?
Purchasing Officer	• Who can supply the equipment? • Where can I get the best price? • What alternatives are available? • How reliable is the supplier? • Can the equipment be easily/cheaply upgraded? • Is it durable? • Is it compatible with existing equipment?
Technician	• How easy is it to repair? • Where can I get the parts? • What does the warranty cover?
Principal	• What will be purchased? • Where will I store it? • What about security? • What are the electrical requirements? • What about safety? • Who will pay for repairs? • Who will pay for replacements?
Teacher	• What training do I need? • How will students use it? • How will teachers use it? • Will the students find it easy to use? • How often will the students use it? • Where will I put it? • Will I need special furniture? • What training will the students need? • Is there a variety of ways in which the equipment can be used?

No matter what hardware you select, be prepared for something faster, easier to use, or with greater capabilities to soon appear on the market. The goal of providing the latest and best hardware for students is constantly challenged by memory upgrades, special features, improvements in speed and portability, and greater compatibility with other technologies. This should not concern you too much, provided that your plan includes provision for upgrading, improvement, and replacement at regular intervals. Remind all involved that exposure to *any* hardware is still valuable, as it advances your intent of strengthening general technological competence.

Computers

Business partnerships, government grants, financial constraints, and personal preferences tend to be the factors governing what kind of computers are used in schools. The day will come when, once you have learned to use a computer, what you have learned will be applicable to most other brands of computers. Indeed, this has already begun to occur, so the time invested in learning to use one type of computer is not lost when you switch to another machine. Before selecting a particular computer, however, speak to a number of suppliers and other educators. In addition to the general hardware considerations previously listed, ask yourself the following questions:

- Is this computer reliable? Speak with others who use this brand.
- How easy is it to use? Think of the age of your students and every step that they must take, from turning on the machine to accessing programs.
- Will you need to move it regularly? Portable computers are constantly improving and becoming less expensive.
- Is color important? Many programs use color effectively but you must be able to justify the extra cost.
- Has the manual been written in a clear, concise fashion? Both beginners and experienced users can benefit from a really good manual.
- Can more memory be added as required? In the future, you may want to integrate CD-ROM drives, modems, or sound boards, so plan ahead.

■ Breaking ground in the use of multimedia does not have to be prohibitively expensive. . . . The first place to look for equipment is in your school's existing inventory. The already-owned television monitor, videocassette recorder, camcorder, personal computer, telephone, and stereo system all can contribute to a basic setup, sometimes with little or no additional purchasing required.[3]

The choice of computer platform often has little relevance to the successful integration of technology into the daily school life of students, provided that the computers can do what you want them to do. Therefore, when selecting which computers to buy, consider the capabilities required. What kind of applications will you most often use?

KINDS OF APPLICATIONS	USED FOR
conferences	• brainstorming • issues, debates • distance learning
computer-assisted instruction	• skill development • knowledge acquisition • individualization
databases	• organizing information • sorting information • examining trends • finding the highest, lowest, biggest, best, etc.
desktop publishing	• newspapers • newsletters • advertising • notices
drill and practice	• mathematics basic facts • spelling and phonics • rote tasks
graphics utilities	• illustrations • drawings • sketches, diagrams, maps • visual communication • visual learning • drafting • design
multimedia	• student and teacher presentations • organizing resources • research • thinking skills • communication skills • creativity
programming and control technologies	• thinking skills • problem solving • enrichment • creativity
simulations	• exploration, discovery • dangerous experiments • topics unable to be explored in the school setting • imaginary topics • identifying with the past, future
spreadsheets	• calculating • tracking costs or scores • statistics • lab results, calculations • tables, graphs, charts • student marks • self-directed learning

telecommunications	• communicating outside the classroom
	• audio- and videoconferencing
	• research
	• distance education
	• accessing experts
word processing	• writing, self-expression
	• notices, letters, bulletins
	• overheads
	• posters, banners
	• tests, handouts

■ Remember to keep the focus on how students can use the technology rather than what the technology can do. The role of the technology is simply to enable human performance. It is more important to be able to say, "My students are great because they have learned to send prepared datafiles via the system," than to say, "The system is great because it lets my students send prepared datafiles."[4]

After deciding which classroom applications you plan to use, you will have a basis on which to select computer hardware. We will look at these applications in greater detail in the next chapter, "Making It Work."

The next question that comes to mind after "What kind of computers?" is often "How many computers?" Teachers have invariably answered that they could never have too many computers, only too little physical space for them! Economics will probably limit teachers' dreams of a computer for every student in every class for a very long time. In the average classroom of 25 to 35 students, we believe that four or five computers is a very good start.

■ Consider this scenario, in which having five computers in a class allows about two hours of computer time per student per week. Mr. Preston teaches a class of 30 students. These students spend a total of 1500 minutes per week in school. If all five computers were used by the students during every minute of every school day, each student would get 250 minutes per week of computer time. We know that this is not the case, nor should it be, since a variety of activities and approaches is important for learning. Reality suggests that about half of Mr. Preston's time with his students is spent in whole-group lessons, activities outside of the classroom, special events, and pursuits for which a computer is neither required nor desirable. (This does not preclude another teacher or other students from using Mr. Preston's computers at these times.) Thus, it is reasonable to estimate that each of Mr. Preston's students has access to about 125 minutes of computer time per week.

Many schools have chosen to network their technologically integrated classrooms to a central fileserver. LAN is the term often used when referring to a local area network. It refers to a group of computers that are physically wired together. They can be in the same room or building, or on the same campus. LANs do not require modems for computers to communicate with one another; instead, they use appropriate LAN interface cards. One computer, called the server, manages the network. The advantages of a network are:

- financial savings due to shared drives and printers;
- with a site license, only one copy of each program is required;
- students can choose from a menu without the teacher having to find individual disks;
- students do not require a disk to save work;
- allows for sharing of data;
- students have the ability to communicate with one another;
- teachers can control screens and demonstrate on screen;
- users require less training than if they had to manage a computer desktop and handle individual disks;
- one person within a school is usually responsible for maintaining the hardware and updating and supporting software.

There are also some disadvantages:

- one problem can bring down the whole system;
- space is required for a fileserver;
- more training is required for the system manager;
- computers are generally slower, especially during start-up periods when many users are logging on simultaneously;
- access to software is limited to those programs loaded on the central fileserver unless each workstation also has its own drive(s).

Printers

At least one printer in the classroom is essential. Students need ready access to their printed work and should not have to leave the room to get it. The noise of a dot matrix printer can be annoying but it is amazing how quickly students and teachers adapt to it as a part of the hum of a busy workplace. As the cost of laser and ink-jet printers declines, their use in classrooms will increase due to the quality of the final product and the quieter operation. If possible, one color printer that can be shared by everyone in the school for special projects is a great addition to your equipment.

Liquid crystal display tablet (LCD tablet)

An LCD tablet is a projection panel that, when placed on top of an overhead projector, allows you to show the computer image on a wall screen. It simply attaches to the computer with a cable, in place of the monitor. With a tablet, you can use the computer for whole-group lessons because the image is large enough for all to see. The high price of LCD tablets, especially color ones, puts them out of reach for many schools. A large school might consider purchasing a few LCD tablets for shared use.

Furniture

Special tables to accommodate computers and printers allow for more efficient organization of work areas. With the simple modification of large holes drilled through the tables, the many power cords and connecting cables can be bundled onto a lower shelf out of sight. School custodians will appreciate the fact that cords are kept off the floor, allowing their brooms to pass under the furniture unobstructed. Another alternative is to have built-in shelving or counters specifically for equipment.

Mobile computer workstations provide the most flexibility but tend to be expensive.

Tables with shelves are practical. Printer paper can feed from underneath.

Fixed counters are relatively permanent, so their locations should be chosen carefully.

Modems and telephone lines

Telecommunications devices are rapidly becoming a tool not only for business but also for educators. In its simplest form, telecommunications is the process of using your computer, a modem, and specific software to communicate over standard telephone lines with other similarly equipped computers. With telecommunications, information can flow in and out of the classroom without interrupting routines and lessons, and the computer can store the information until you are ready to work with it.

Modems are not expensive; speed is the factor that affects price. The most common speed of modems has been 2400 bits/second (baud) but with today's constantly improving technology, you would be wise to consider purchasing a 4800- or 9600-baud modem.

■ The word modem derives from modulate/demodulate. At one end, the modem modulates the digital signals generated by a computer into analog tones that can be transmitted along telephone lines. At the other end of the telecommunications link, the modem demodulates the analog tones back into the digital signals that the computer requires. This allows users to send messages and communicate on-screen through their computers. The process of transferring information from a host computer to a user is called downloading. A user can download a variety of text or graphics, save them, and/or print them.

Access to a telephone line in a school is often the biggest stumbling block in implementing telecommunications. Despite the fact that approximately 99% of households have one, a telephone line into a classroom has, in the past, not been considered necessary. Thus, a telephone line dedicated to telecommunications has been a luxury that many schools have believed they could not afford. As more and more individuals and institutions access the information networks, however, a communications line becomes essential. Without a dedicated line, you may be limited to having students prepare their messages during school hours for you to send later in the evening when a telephone line is available. This compromise is a burden to teachers and deprives students of the opportunity to experience telecommunicating firsthand. To take full advantage of telecommunications, classrooms require access to a modem and a telephone line.

■ Educators spend much of their time discussing educational issues with onsite colleagues, reading professional journals, and searching for new approaches and ideas. "More teacher time is spent networking for professional development than in the context of teaching. The major incentive for networking is the isolation teachers feel in their profession."[5]

The potential of telecommunications for education is obvious in the burgeoning field of distance learning. Although you may not yet be involved or contemplating involvement in this specialized field, it is exciting to think of the possibilities ahead, such as audioconferencing, audiographic conferencing, and videoconferencing.

Audioconferencing allows a group of learners to interact, using telephone handsets or speakerphones. Audiographics allows for transmission of graphics at the same time as voice messages, using a standard telephone line. Computers with special software packages and modems are required, and an electronic tablet and pen can be used to write or draw on-line. With the appropriate software, you can add computer-generated text and graphics, video clips, photos, and scanned images.

Videoconferencing involves the transmission of full images and sound. In other words, a group of learners at one site can see and speak with learners at another, using cameras and TV screens. The audio and video are transmitted using a large number of telephone lines.[6] Electronic highways are the channels on which knowledge travels, in digital format, to other destinations.

■ Predictions regarding advances in telecommunications networks suggest that they will soon become capable of much more than simply communication of text: ". . . baud-width will soon be almost free. The KDD-AT&T fiberoptic cable to Japan is running at 4 billion bits per second (all 32 volumes of the *Encyclopedia Britannica*, including pictures, can be sent in 6 seconds flat!). We will soon see 56K baud lines the way we see 2400 baud today. The real beauty of this is that we'll ship animation, voice and data as easily as we now send text."[7]

Audio equipment

Studies have shown that students spend nearly 50% of their classroom time listening, yet most schools offer no formal classes in listening.[8] Audio equipment is used to address the needs of those students who learn best by listening, to remediate weak listening skills, to support written text, and to enhance student presentations.

Although many computers now integrate audio input and/or output, students in a technology-integrated classroom also find it useful to have access to a large tape recorder, as well as to the smaller, hand-held variety.

Larger tape recorders are suitable for groups as they listen to stories, newspaper articles, poems, or musical selections. The smaller, hand-held variety is ideal for speaking activities, as well as for individual assignments such as review of addition facts.

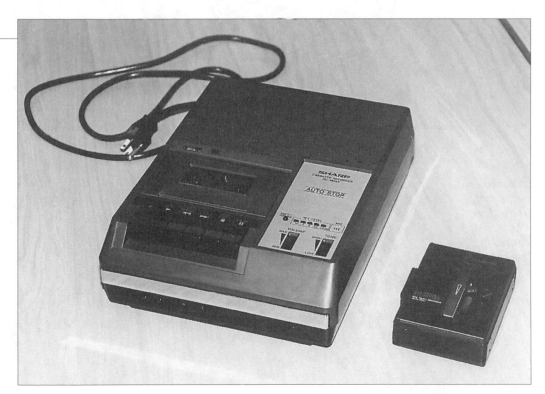

Avoid special features on tape recorders, such as voice activation, unless they are required for a specific purpose, as too many controls and special features can present problems, especially for younger children. Battery-operated, hand-held tape recorders give students the flexibility to move to where they can quietly do a speaking activity or perhaps an interview. The most obvious disadvantage of small technology such as this is its relatively short life span. If damaged or dropped, repair may not be financially worthwhile. With adequate care, however, these small tape recorders can give students two or three years (and sometimes longer) of trouble-free use.

Audiocassette tapes have been used in many classrooms for a number of years. You can record cassettes yourself or buy commercial productions. Be aware of copyright laws when making your own tapes for classroom use. To prevent the accidental erasing of these selections, simply break the plastic clip at the top of each cassette. Re-cover the hole with tape if you want to erase work. Audiocassette tapes are inexpensive and can be used to develop many important skills; they can be used many times over. Even very young children can use this technology with the greatest of ease.

Headphones are *essential* when using any kind of audio equipment in the busy classroom environment. When headphones are used for a variety of equipment, teachers and students quickly discover that some pieces of equipment require a large plug, while others require a small one. Adapters sound like the answer but they are small and quickly lost. A better solution is to provide headphones with a variety of sizes of plugs.

Small headphones may survive for a year or so, but they cannot stand long-term, constant use. Good-quality headphones will help you to maintain a quieter work environment.

Many companies will customize headphones to suit your needs. For example, in this illustration, the plugs have been changed to fit different pieces of equipment.

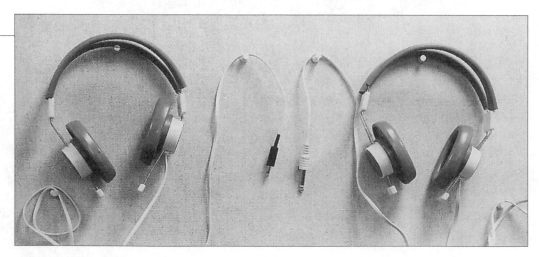

Audiovisual equipment

TV/VCR

A combination TV/VCR can be used for whole-class, small-group, and individual viewing. One of the advantages to selecting a combination unit is its portability, an important consideration when teachers share equipment. Also, combination TV/VCRs have fewer wires; thus, there are fewer connections to be made.

TV/VCR units can be purchased with either vertical or horizontal loading. With younger students in mind, horizontal loading is the logical choice because it is the type with which children are most familiar. Most units wisely have the fine-tuning controls out of sight, but find out where they are located in case students decide to experiment! A TV/VCR can be adapted for headphones by the simple addition of a jack and switch. The jack is required for the attachment of headphones, while the switch is used to switch the audio back and forth from the headphones to the speakers.

CD-ROM

The CD-ROM (compact disc–read-only memory) is one of the most popular technologies being used in education today. Whereas a music CD stores only audio information, a CD-ROM can digitally store both visual and audio information. The plastic disc, 12 cm in diameter, looks the same as a music CD. A single CD-ROM can hold 650 megabytes of computer information — approximately 250 000 single-spaced, keyed pages. The information on a CD-ROM is permanent and cannot be changed. CD-ROM is popular because the discs last for years; large quantities of information are available in the form of databases, encyclopedias, and atlases; and information access is quick and easy.

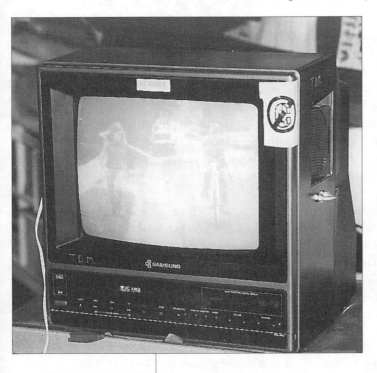

The combination TV/VCR takes up very little space in the typically crowded classroom.

A technician can add an audio jack and switch so that the unit can be used with headphones. At the same time, add a U-bolt so that the equipment can be secured to a table or wall. Always check with the manufacturer before opening the casing; otherwise, the warranty might be invalidated.

■ **THE TEXTBOOK IS DEAD!** [9]

ENCYCLOPEDIA	CD-ROM
• unlimited text and pictures	• 275 000 pages or combination of text, pictures, sound, video
• costs $500 to print	• costs $1.50 to print
• takes 15 hours to print	• takes 6 seconds to manufacture
• weighs 1100 kg	• weighs 17 g
• takes 23 trees to produce	• made of 16 g of polycarbonate and 1 mg of aluminum
• access in hours using sneakers	• any word or phrase in 3 seconds
• single pathway — left to right, top to bottom, beginning, to end	• multiple pathways constructed by the learner
• text and pictures	• textual, pictorial, sound, film, animations, computer programs
• $800 or more each time	• under $1000 for encyclopedia and player; updated annually

CD-ROM drives can be external or built into the computer. A computer with a built-in CD-ROM drive has fewer cables and is easier to set up and move. When making your computer purchase, ensure it has sufficient memory that the many features of different CDs can be accessed. By examining some of the CD-ROM discs that will be your first purchases, you can find out how much memory and what special features will be required by the computer to run them (e.g., type of monitor, CD-ROM drive).

Some of the most valuable features of CDs available today include audio segments, visual components such as charts and graphs, and video segments. For example, one CD-ROM encyclopedia of mammals allows students to read information about the animal they select, see still photos, watch a brief video clip of the animal's movements or feeding habits, and hear the sound it makes. A world atlas on CD-ROM locates the country selected, displays a short video of the landscape, provides graphs of features such as climate and population, plays the national anthem of the country, and more. Many CDs allow the student to place electronic bookmarks so they can return to specific points later, make notes, access cross-referencing, and use a dictionary and glossary.

Electronic books allow for a level of interactivity not possible in conventional books. With multimedia authoring software, explained in more detail in Chapter 4, "Making It Work," they can be made dynamic and reactive, using animation, sound effects, simulations, and windows that embed text, static pictures, and/or video clips. The numerous CDs available provide a multitude of learning opportunities, provided that you have the hardware capabilities to use them.

Videodisc player

Videodisc players can be an exciting part of the interactive instructional system. They can be used to enhance large-group presentations or as a research tool for small groups or individual students. Their most attractive features include the excellent quality of the image and the flexible use of content that are possible. The interactive capabilities of videodisc players make them far superior to VCRs, although they may cost up to twice as much.

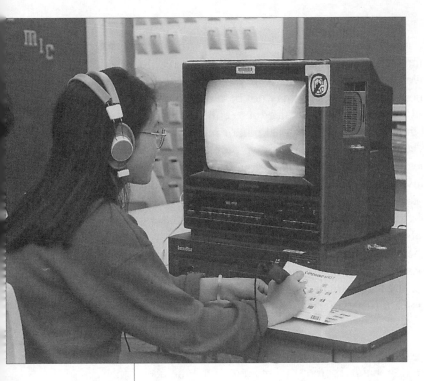

Unlike video, no tedious rewinding is necessary. Bar codes allow the teacher to move immediately to a particular image or video clip to demonstrate a concept or stimulate discussion. Many videodisc packages come with what are called bar-coded lesson guides. The student working independently can also move to any spot on the disc with a touch of the bar-code reader.

The use of videodisc is limited by the type of player; therefore, when purchasing a videodisc player, explore its capabilities to make sure that it will suit your needs. You may require the assistance of a technical adviser, because different manufacturers classify videodisc players in different ways.

Bar-code readers are easy to use. Bar codes are groups of optically coded parallel lines, such as those commonly used on grocery items. By scanning the reader across the code, students can quickly move to various points on the videodisc.

Figure 3.2

Some manufacturers designate videodisc players by levels, according to their capabilities; the definitions of these levels may vary somewhat from one manufacturer to another, so be careful.

Levels of Videodisc Players	
Level	**Capabilities**
Basic	• play discs from beginning to end with no scheduled interruptions
Level 1	• step or scan forward or backward • go to a particular chapter or frame • freeze frame • change the speed of motion
Level 2	• operate through a computer equipped with a serial interface card • software can allow access by chapter, time, or frame • software can enable note-making while viewing • material can be transferred into multimedia presentations
Level 3	• one or more videodiscs interface with computer • complex software for graphics, explanations, problems, open-ended questions • tools such as light pens, joysticks, paddles, touch screens can be used for input • may use two monitors, one displaying videodisc information and the other computer information or may display both on the same screen

Other equipment

Students and teachers can find many uses for a video camera. As you explore the possibilities, you may discover that some students are already quite comfortable with the operation of a video camera. A video camera may not be required on a daily basis, but it is great to have access to one when students need it to enhance multimedia presentations, collect visual data, practice public speaking, or prepare news broadcasts and dramas. Keep durability and portability in mind when purchasing a video camera for classroom use. Select special features according to your anticipated uses of the camera. A tripod is a good investment that may add years to the life of your video camera.

Equipment does not have to be large or costly to be useful. Calculators are a good example. Younger students also enjoy using a spell checker when writing, proofreading, or editing. They enter a phonetic or approximated spelling of a word and the spell checker provides a list of possible words from which the student selects the one required. When budgeting for the technological classroom, do not forget the other important ingredients such as batteries, battery chargers, adapters, power bars, extension cords, security cables, and locks.

■ It was a pleasure to see how naturally the students integrated the use of the computer, desktop VCR, hand-held tape recorders, and other equipment into units of study. (Sharon Anderson and Laurie DiLabio, teachers)]

Advice from experienced technicians

If you are responsible for making the final decision about which piece(s) of equipment to purchase, you will want to know what to do when your equipment requires service and what the warranties on your equipment will cover. We asked the opinions of two experienced technicians who have successfully maintained and supported technological classrooms for the past five years. The following questions and answers may help to guide you.

Q. What do warranties cover?

A. Warranties mainly cover the manufacturer's defects anywhere from 90 days to two years. They are usually for one or two years. A warranty does not cover repair required due to abuse or accident. Usually, a warranty repair will occur in the first 30 days but audiovisual equipment failure is rare; in fact, within our school system, only 2% or 3% required a warranty claim. The purchaser must keep the bill of sale for the equipment: if it is lost, the company could base the warranty coverage on the manufacturing date, but this would result in the loss of valuable warranty coverage.

The receipt also usually contains information that could be valuable to you in discussing the product with the manufacturer or supplier. It is important to remember that physically opening the equipment usually voids the warranty. If you are planning to attach a U-bolt to the equipment for security purposes, you would be well advised to check with the company to see if it will affect your warranty. As for computers, the best advice we can give is to sit down with the salesperson and make sure that you know what is covered under warranty. Does it cover parts and service and, if so, over what period of time? Make sure that you know what factors will void your warranty.

Q. What is the difference between consumer and industrial equipment?

A. Consumer equipment is manufactured for the home market while industrial equipment comes with industrial certification. Because industrial equipment is more durable and, thus, more expensive, most schools cannot afford their purchases to be totally of industrially certified equipment. As the purchaser, you will need to check if the consumer equipment used in your classroom will be covered under warranty.

Q. What type of service system would you recommend?

A. There are three options for servicing of equipment: you can enter into a service contract with a dealer who is authorized to perform repairs under warranty; you can go to a third-party service company or repair depot; or you may decide to invest in the services of a technician for your school system.

The authorized dealer can provide proper servicing for your equipment, and for many small systems of education, this may be most practical. Third-party service can look attractive, but may not guarantee quick availability of authorized parts. Try to have another service organization available in the event that one cannot fulfill your needs.

The best option may be a system technician. Such a staff member can provide preventative maintenance, may know of temporary alternative arrangements, can expedite the service process when necessary, and can have spare parts on hand. Another advantage of an in-house technician is that school equipment can be readily repaired, rather than sitting on a shelf until money becomes available. Within our system of about 40 schools, an average number of 500 pieces of equipment were repaired annually when equipment was serviced by an outside company. This figure jumped to 750 per annum when there was a technician available to do preventative maintenance on a regular basis. This means that more equipment is always available for student use.

Q. What are the typical problems associated with audiovisual equipment?

A. With audiovisual equipment, three main problems occur: videotapes and audiotapes jam in the machines, equipment not regularly cleaned ceases to function, and damage results from equipment being dropped. It is so important to teach the students the proper care and use of the technology!

Q. What are the typical problems associated with computer equipment?

A. Computer problems are generally more complex. The first step is to determine if it is a hardware or software problem. In computers, the common problems occur with the monitor, the motherboard, interface cards, drives, and power supply. Your supplier should have a service department and should be a resource for you. You need experts to support you.

Q. What advice would you give teachers when they are purchasing equipment?

A. Buy brand names. The brand-name manufacturers have trained technicians. They have a vested interest and will want you to buy their product again. Be sure the equipment you select is durable. The system of education for which you work usually has a tender list: consult it before purchasing. Consider a plan for the rotational replacement of the equipment. Be sure that the equipment suits your needs. If it is too complicated, the students will encounter difficulties in using it. Think about what it is you want your students to do with the equipment before you buy it. This is particularly important when selecting a computer: remember, it is the software that makes it work!

CHAPTER 4

Making It Work

The hardware is always ahead of the software, and the software (tools) always ahead of the educational applications.[1]

Facing a room filled with technology at the beginning of a new school year can be a more overwhelming experience than facing a roomful of students! Questions come to mind, such as: "What will I actually do with all of this? What software is available? How will I choose the best and most appropriate technological learning materials for my students?" One teacher described her initial experiences this way:

Boxes of equipment had been arriving — computers, a videodisc player, a computer with CD-ROM, a VCR. We couldn't wait any longer to begin setting up. It was so exciting! I asked a few of my 12-year-old students to help me out and we started to organize the room. At first, I used any learning materials and computer software that I could get my hands on. Our school didn't have a great selection yet but I wanted the students to use the technology right away and to see what it could do. As the year went on, I became more selective about software. If there was a print or audiovisual resource that fit my learning objectives better, I could always find a use for the computers, such as word processing or graphics creation. I learned a lot about what learning materials were available from talking with other teachers.

In reading this chapter, consider technological learning materials as including more than just computer software. The value of each piece of hardware depends on the pedagogy and content of the materials you use with it; this includes videotapes, CD-ROM discs, videodiscs, etc. Teachers cannot be expected to be aware of the complete line of materials that are being added to the market on a daily basis. You can best stay informed about new materials specific to your needs by attending workshops, consulting resource personnel in your school or school system, reading journals, and talking to your peers.

Once you have access to bulletin boards, local networks, the Internet, or any of the commercial on-line services, you will have many ways to find out both what is available and about the options and experiences of other teachers. Some examples of these services are CompuServe, America Online, Dow Jones News/Retrieval, GEnie, and Prodigy.

Rather than attempting to provide lengthy lists of recommended materials, we have chosen to look at the relevant criteria for selecting technological learning materials to enhance your curriculum. We also consider the various educational applications of different types of software for students. In Chapter 10, "Tools for Teachers," we discuss how teachers can use software for their own tasks.

Computer software

The quality of early educational software was poor. In 1983, the Educational Products Information Exchange reviewed and rated available educational software and identified only 5% of programs as "highly recommended."[2] Software was authored either by educators who were new to programming or by programming experts who lacked knowledge about the curriculum and how children learn. Despite the fact that developers have since learned more about education and educators about development, it is still not a good practice to order software sight unseen. Try to obtain a demo disk or, better yet, the complete disk. Some software companies may be reluctant to send a complete disk for preview. If you come up against this obstacle, Geisert and Futrell[3] recommend the following strategies when writing for software to preview:

- Use school letterhead.
- Request only one or two titles at a time.
- State the instructional objectives for the software.
- State that you will be personally responsible for the software.
- Assume responsibility for returning it on time.
- State that you will supply a brief explanation if you decide not to purchase the software.

Evaluation of software is becoming an important factor in the continuing education of teachers. Before investing a lot of time developing your own evaluation criteria, find out if your school or school system has already adopted an evaluation procedure. Consult experts and curriculum specialists, if they are available. In many cases, software is recommended by a review committee and purchased centrally by school systems. If you prefer to do your own evaluation, simply decide what criteria you want to use and find or develop a good evaluation form. You know your students and objectives best. Educational journals and magazines are also good sources of software evaluation criteria. Common criteria include:

- Instructional quality:
    - What mode of instruction is used?
    - Does it reflect good pedagogy?
    - Are goals and objectives clearly stated?
    - Are thinking skills part of the objectives?
    - Is the content appropriate?
    - Is there a variety of problems?

- Production quality:
    - Is the quality of the graphics and sound acceptable or better?
    - Does it have prompt and appropriate feedback?
    - Is material presented in a clear and logical sequence?

- Flexibility:
  - Is it easy to use?
  - Are there levels of difficulty or can the program be modified to address student needs?
  - Is it suitable for a cooperative learning environment?
  - Is it accompanied by useful documentation?
  - Can it be used for self-study?

- Cost:
  - How many students will benefit?
  - Does it utilize available computer capabilities?
  - Will additional peripherals be needed?

By using the software evaluation checklist shown in Blackline Master 4.1, "What Do You Think?" you could involve your students in the selection process. Blackline Master 4.2 on pages 42 and 43 provides a more detailed software evaluation checklist for your use.

One way to learn about new software is by scanning reviews in education magazines, journals, and books. Some reviewers have a vested interest in promoting specific software, so take into account the reviewer's qualifications, educational and/or technical expertise, and if he or she has actually tried the software with students. A more time-efficient way to learn about new software might be to access a special-interest group through a telecommunications network. This allows you to communicate directly with other teachers who have used a piece of software and share their experiences.

How you plan to use the software to support your curriculum is the final determining factor. The following are some common software applications and how and why they might be useful to students.

Word processing

Speed, power, and ease of revision make writing on the computer more productive than using pencil and paper. Students adapt easily to composing on-screen once they become used to it and often resist returning to "old-fashioned" writing tools. Manual skills continue to be necessary, however, and should not be ignored. When using word processing, the focus can be on the writing process — prewriting, composing, revising, and editing — not just on the content. Many students experience increased self-esteem due to the professional appearance of their completed work, especially those with poor manual skills. Students also enjoy having their collected works readily accessible in their portfolios.

Every computer has word processing software and each package is unique. Consider ease of use for the particular age range of students and invest some time in teaching students how to effectively use the features available. Special features are more important for older students, but all students benefit from features such as:

- spell check;
- grammar check;
- glossary;
- on-line help.

BLM 4.1

What Do You Think?

Check Yes ___ or No ___

1. Did you understand the directions?   Yes ___ No ___

2. Can you use this program easily?   Yes ___ No ___

3. Was the text easy to read?   Yes ___ No ___

4. Do you like the graphics (pictures)?   Yes ___ No ___

5. Are there sound effects?   Yes ___ No ___

6. Did you like the sounds?   Yes ___ No ___

7. Did the program tell you immediately if your
   answer was right or wrong?   Yes ___ No ___
   - or -
   Did it give you the information you wanted?   Yes ___ No ___

8. Was the program too easy?   Yes ___ No ___

9. Was it too difficult?   Yes ___ No ___

10. Would you like to use this program again?   Yes ___ No ___

Comments: _____

_____

_____

_____

BLM 4.1

Software Evaluation Checklist

Program Title _____

Package Title _____

Cost _____ Copyright Date _____

Publisher _____

Address _____

Required Hardware _____

Prerequisite Skills _____

....

Rate the software using the following key: Y: Yes N: No N/A: Not Applicable

Documentation

Hardware requirements are clearly stated.   Y ___   N ___   N/A ___

Program installation is easy to follow.   Y ___   N ___   N/A ___

Goals/objectives are clearly defined.   Y ___   N ___   N/A ___

Teaching ideas/suggestions and/or
 additional activities are provided.   Y ___   N ___   N/A ___

Prerequisite skills have been stated.   Y ___   N ___   N/A ___

Operating of Software

Instructions are clear.   Y ___   N ___   N/A ___

Help screens are provided throughout the
 program.   Y ___   N ___   N/A ___

Screen display is well designed.   Y ___   N ___   N/A ___

Software is reliable and free of bugs.   Y ___   N ___   N/A ___

Student controls the pace.   Y ___   N ___   N/A ___

Student can exit the software at any time.   Y ___   N ___   N/A ___

Students can re-enter the program where
 they stopped.   Y ___   N ___   N/A ___

Student can access previous screens.   Y ___   N ___   N/A ___

continued...

BLM 4.2 (cont'd)

Presentation

Reading level is appropriate for the intended
audience.   Y ____   N ____   N/A ____

Sound enhances the program.   Y ____   N ____   N/A ____

Graphics are appropriate.   Y ____   N ____   N/A ____

Feedback is immediate and motivating.   Y ____   N ____   N/A ____

Feedback after an incorrect response is
immediate and helpful.   Y ____   N ____   N/A ____

Content

Content is accurate.   Y ____   N ____   N/A ____

Content is free of biases/stereotypes.   Y ____   N ____   N/A ____

Content reflects the objectives.   Y ____   N ____   N/A ____

Content is suitable for the intended audience.   Y ____   N ____   N/A ____

Content is presented in blocks.   Y ____   N ____   N/A ____

Content is presented in a variety of ways.   Y ____   N ____   N/A ____

Management

Student records are saved.   Y ____   N ____   N/A ____

Clear reports are provided on student
achievement.   Y ____   N ____   N/A ____

Student records are private.   Y ____   N ____   N/A ____

Teachers can access records easily.   Y ____   N ____   N/A ____

Recommendation

Excellent ____ Good ____ Fair ____ Poor ____

Databases

A database is simply a collection of organized data that the user can manipulate using the computer. In this information generation, students no longer need to memorize data; rather, they must know how to gather, organize, analyze, and retrieve data. The creation and use of databases is a skill transferable to the world outside the classroom, since much of the information available to us is collected and stored in the form of databases. Databases can be used in many subject areas. The creation and use of databases become relevant to students when they take place in a curriculum context, for example:

- As a part of an ecology unit, students develop a database of endangered species of their country, using fields such as habitat, size, mass, food, and color.
- Each student researches a different country and adds information about size, population, languages, capital city, etc., to a class database.
- Students create an historical time-line by entering events with their dates and locations and then sorting them into chronological order.
- Students organize baseball or hockey card collections according to each athlete's name, team, position played, years of experience, age, and salary.
- Students at each school collect and sort the school's garbage on a given day. The data is sent to a central location, where it is entered into a database representing the whole system. The complete database is returned to all schools for various types of analysis.
- Students use a climate database to research and graph predicted temperatures and precipitation over several months, and then measure and compare these to the actual climate.

Virtually any computer can run a database program but some software is superior to others. Consider ease of student use when selecting database software — entering, altering, and sorting data should be straightforward for students to learn. If your students have never used a database, begin by having them work with a ready-made database before expecting them to create their own. Within a few months of being exposed to databases, even quite young students will readily use them as a format for collecting all kinds of data. Older students will quickly see the value of learning relevant vocabulary such as grid, record, field, and cell. The creation of databases teaches students to make judgments about what data is important and relevant to the topic. They develop an understanding of the ways in which data must be presented and the ways in which computers can work with data. The opportunities for gathering, organizing, manipulating, and storing information make larger quantities of information manageable by students of all ages. Databases also empower students to analyze and synthesize greater amounts of information within their own interests.

■ The first year, eight year olds were introduced to the power of collecting and sorting data by collecting a class database. Each child, with the help of a teacher, recorded data such as favorite book, color of eyes, hair color, number of siblings, etc. After everyone in the class of approximately 60 students recorded information it was time to let them experience the ease with which this data could be manipulated. They delighted in seeing the computer search for and list all the children with a given trait. It's quite a thrill to be able to print out all your classmates who love pizza or a list of everyone who is also an only child.[4]

Desktop publishing

Desktop publishing is a popular term used to describe a word processing system that integrates text and graphics. Older students particularly need access to good desktop publishing software. They can use it to produce flyers, posters, newsletters, newspapers, yearbooks, etc. Some advantages to using a computer for these kinds of tasks are:

- speed;
- ease of revision;
- professional appearance;
- motivation.

You can buy desktop publishing software simple enough for even young students to learn. However, desktop publishing introduces students to real-world technology, provides a purposeful application of language skills, and can be used to create a powerful link between the school and the community. When selecting desktop publishing software, ask yourself:

- What are my students' needs?
- Will the students be able to use it easily?
- Is it compatible with the existing word processing software?
- What features are offered?

Drill and practice

Because drill and practice software is specific for subject, age level, and skill, we can consider it only in general terms. Its purpose is to improve student performance in a specific task or skill. Look for these characteristics in drill and practice software:

- different skill levels;
- modifiable for students with special needs;
- teacher-controlled input and options;
- students able to create their own tasks and tasks for others;
- relevant and immediate feedback;
- built-in motivation;
- self-directed and self-paced;
- on-line help;
- attractive graphics;
- randomly generated questions;
- teacher access to students' work;
- helpful support materials.

Computer-assisted instruction

Computer-assisted instruction facilitates the learning of specific skills and/or knowledge through a lesson or series of lessons. These lessons are often followed by practice sessions and tests. Interactivity, immediate feedback, and the use of mastery learning principles are important elements of good computer-assisted learning software. Often called courseware, computer-assisted instruction has a variety of potential applications: whole-group instruction, small-group teaching, review, remediation, enrichment, and individualization of student programs.

You need frequent access to a computer lab if you want to use computer-assisted instruction as a main component of your unit or course of study, but two or three computers are adequate for review, remediation, or enrichment purposes. To take advantage of on-screen lessons for whole-group teaching, an LCD tablet or other projection device is required. The important features of drill and practice software mentioned above also apply to computer-assisted instruction software.

Graphics utilities

Students require software that allows them to design and also to create pictures and diagrams such as the ones on page 46. They can use graphics in daily tasks and will inevitably encounter computer technology as a part of future arts courses. Computer

Sample computer graphics by a student in the 6–8 age group.

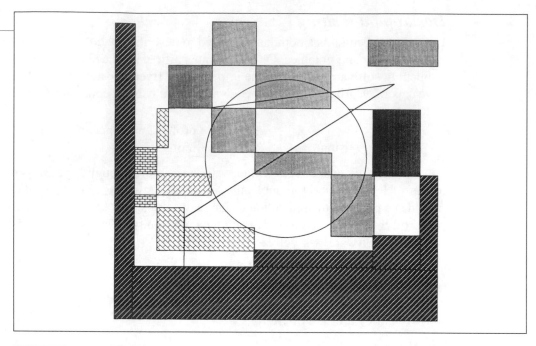

Sample computer graphics by a student in the 9–11 age group.

Sample computer graphics by a student in the 12–14 age group.

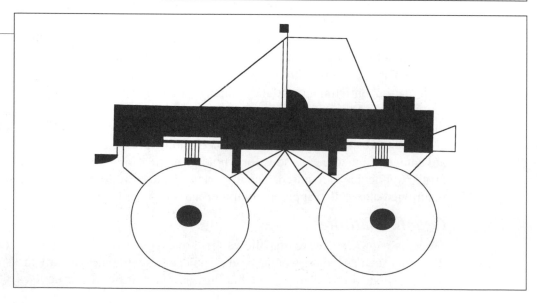

graphics are becoming part of the professional's toolbox in many areas such as commercial art, interior design, mass communications, and media production.

Using a graphics program, students have at their disposal a variety of color palettes and designs with which they can experiment before using traditional tools and materials. They can work with points, lines, planes, and perspective. They can manipulate existing images that have been captured with a video camera or scanner in order to experiment with foreground and background and the use of perspective.

Graphics programs vary from simple to very complex — your choice depends on the users and your goals. A color monitor makes graphics creation much more exciting, but if you do not also have a color printer, it might be better to leave the image stored in the computer. Students may be disappointed when they see their printout in shades of gray.

Programming and control technologies

Programming provides a medium for developing thinking skills, exploring, experimenting, and problem solving. When students program, they are able to create and control applications, as opposed to being at the mercy of commercial software. Logo is a popular programming language created for children. It was developed by Seymour Papert at the Massachusetts Institute of Technology in the late 1960s, following his long association with Jean Piaget. Logo views learners as the builders of their own knowledge as they interact with their world. Even preschool children are able to learn simple programming using turtle graphics and this programming language. Logo must be purchased for the appropriate platform and, once loaded, enables students to create graphics; make music; explore ideas in science, mathematics, and language; and control robotic devices.

Programming today can be part of the user's application environment, using text, pictures, sound, and animation. Multimedia platforms, discussed in more detail later in this chapter, allow students to program their own simple or complex presentations. Programming by example is also possible; that is, you show the machine what you want, it records the procedures for you, and you can then change and modify those.

The problem solving that takes place using control technologies can be open-ended exploration, guided investigation of concepts and skills, simulation of real-life

Basic programming allows students to use computers to control machines they build. Commercial construction sets are most often used for these types of activities. A simple, easy-to-use interface provides the communication link between the computer and the student-constructed models.

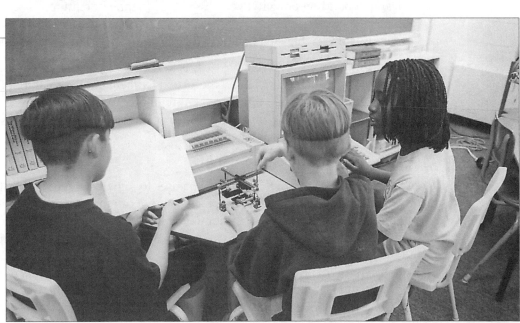

examples, or invention. Construction sets combined with control technologies provide students with a hands-on, problem-solving environment in which they can tackle activities such as the following:

- Design and build a safe, reliable merry-go-round for the fair. It must carry four passengers. Each ride must take a specific length of time and then the merry-go-round must stop to let people off. Music would make the ride more enjoyable!
- You work in a rest home in which the elderly people sometimes leave the bathwater running. Design and build a system to warn that a tap has been left running. Remember that elderly people may be shortsighted and/or hard of hearing.
- Design and build a machine to move pallets in a warehouse. It must be able to pick up a pallet of 10 bricks, move it a distance of 30 cm up a ramp, and place it on the ground next to another pallet.

Students must come to these kinds of activities with a background of problem solving in a technological environment. In a well-designed, sequential design and technology program, computer control is but one aspect in a hierarchy of skills that includes:

- building with soft materials (water, sand, modelling clay);
- building with hard materials (cardboard, plastic, wood, junk, construction kits);
- desire for movement (wheels, pivots, hinges, pulleys);
- motorizing (elastics, balloons, wind, water, electric motors);
- action (lights, bells, pumps);
- control (manual, electric, computer).

Simulations

Computer simulations are useful for exploring concepts that may be too dangerous, complex, expensive, or otherwise impossible within the confines of the classroom. Students might use a simulation to:

- develop and sustain an ecosystem;
- design and build a robot to cross a specific terrain;
- design a building or a city;
- explore a faraway planet;
- manipulate variables in plant growth;
- establish and maintain the economy of a town;
- experience life in a different time or culture;
- plan a trip.

Many such simulations are available — it is a matter of selecting good ones that fit your curriculum. Students are highly motivated by the game-like nature of most simulations, and will happily return to them regularly. While enjoying the activity, students are also developing important skills such as reading, critical thinking, decision making, and problem solving.

Spreadsheets

A spreadsheet is a program that enables the user to organize data into a pattern. When the user adds a formula to the pattern, the changing of numbers results in immediate calculation and adjustment of other numbers. Spreadsheets are used by accountants, financiers, and anyone who needs to balance a budget. Their benefits to students include visibility of large amounts of information, speed, accuracy, organization, and ease of revision. We have seen students as young as eight or nine years old work successfully with spreadsheets. Novice users can begin with an already existing template and progress toward developing spreadsheet formats of their own for specific tasks.

This simple problem-solving spreadsheet activity helps beginners learn to find and edit cell contents. After finding the secret message, the student could devise a secret message for a partner or another team.

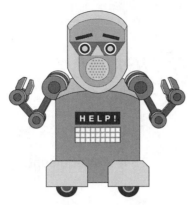

A Secret Message .....
Help!!!!

Robo the robot is lost! It has given you clues, but you must decode its secret message.

All you need to do is follow the instructions IN ORDER, and enter the correct headings for each cell. When you are finished, you will be able to read Robo's message! Good luck!

Cell	Heading	Cell	Heading
1. A1	Dear friends,	16. C11	my site.
2. B9	set me free!	17. A8	If you can find
3. A11	I'll give you	18. C15	and think
4. D6	!!!!!	19. A12	Follow them
5. D12	right!	20. D3	disco is a very
6. B3	land of Floppi-	21. B11	clues to find
7. C14	Then think,	22. A9	Then you will
8. B12	well, make	23. C3	disco. Floppi-
9. B8	my hidden face	24. D17	will set me
10. A3	I'm lost in the	25. C12	sure they are
11. B17	with all your	26. C6	in outer space
12. E19	ROBO	27. C18	FREE !!!!!!
13. B6	I feel as if I'm	28. C8	,
14. A4	funny place!	29. D19	Signed,
15. C17	might! And you		

Answer Key					
	A	**B**	**C**	**D**	**E**
1	Dear friends,				
2					
3	I'm lost in the	land of Floppi-	disco. Floppi-	disco is a very	
4	funny place!				
5					
6		I feel as if I'm	in outer space	!!!!!	
7					
8	If you can find	my hidden face	,		
9	Then you will	set me free!			
10					
11	I'll give you	clues to find	my site.		
12	Follow them	well, make	sure they are	right!	
13					
14			Then think,		
15			and think		
16					
17		with all your	might! And you	will set me	
18			FREE !!!!!!!!		
19				Signed,	ROBO
20					
21					

Reprinted with the permission of Sonja Karsh

With the sales data found on this student activity sheet, the student is asked to program the spreadsheet to calculate the total monthly sales and average weekly sales for the Friendly Grocer store. To do this, students must know how to add, multiply, divide, and calculate an average. They must learn how to enter data, enter headings and titles, add and average cells, and save a file.

ACTIVITY #5

Friendly Grocer

LEVEL: 2

Time Arrangement: Approx. 90 min

Curriculum Skills:
Charting
Creating a template
Averaging numbers
Selecting appropriate notations
Interpreting
Perceiving relationships

Spreadsheet Skills:
Entering data
Averaging cells
Go to function
Entering headings and title
Saving a file
Adding contents of cells

Materials:
Spreadsheet package
Data disk
Student Activity Sheet

Procedure:
With the sales data found on the Student Activity Sheet, the student is asked to program the spreadsheet to calculate the total monthly sales and average weekly sales for the *Friendly Grocer* grocery store.

The student must enter a title and proper headings for the spreadsheet and must know how to add, multiply, divide numbers, and calculate an average.

The results must be reported clearly. When all is tabulated, the student saves the work for you to look at, or prints it if there is an available printer.

Answers

1. Weekly totals: Mar. 5 = $1431.87
    Mar. 12 = $1633.72
    Mar. 19 = $1539.46
    Mar. 26 = $1396.07

2. Monthly total: $6001.12

3. Weekly average: $1500.28

4. $6173.72

5. $1477.87

continued...

... continued

STUDENT ACTIVITY SHEET   Name_____

Friendly Grocer

Your Friendly Grocer *store needs your help! The owner doesn't have a computer, and she needs a monthly report in a hurry! Knowing how fast you are, she wants you to put in the following numbers and answer her questions.*

The *Friendly Grocer* had the following sales:

Week of March 5:   meat: $415.65; produce: $327.00; dairy: $178.97; dry goods: $386.50; bakery: $123.75.

Week of March 12:   meat: $467.53; produce: $345.88; dairy: $206.00; dry goods: $376.25; bakery: $143.80.

Week of March 19:   meat: $524.12; produce: $458.29; dairy: $223.54; dry goods: $290.00; bakery: $137.77.

Week of March 26:   meat: $398.00; produce: $366.40; dairy: $187.68; dry goods: $287.99; bakery: $156.00.

Questions

1. On your spreadsheet, indicate each of the weekly totals (sales for all departments). Be sure to make the computer calculate the answer! Use cell names in your formulas, NOT numbers!

   Weekly totals: Mar. 5 =   Mar. 19 =

   Mar. 12 =   Mar. 26 =

2. On your spreadsheet, show the monthly total for all departments.

   Monthly total: _____

3. On your spreadsheet, calculate and show the weekly average for the month of March.

   Weekly average: _____

4. What would be the new monthly total if the dairy amount was $378.60 for the week of March 12?

   _____

5. What would be the new weekly average if the dairy amount was $378.60 for the week of March 12, if the meat department amount was $309.41 for the week of March 5, and if the bakery had been closed for repairs the week of March 26?

   _____

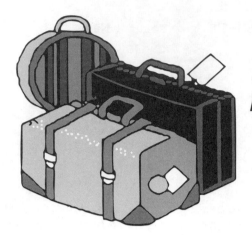

Using the spreadsheet motivates students to practice the skills of map reading and calculating distance using a scale.

ACTIVITY #6

Keeping Track of Travel

LEVEL: 2   **Time Arrangement:** Approx. 90 min

Curriculum Skills: Reading a map
Calculating kilometric distance from a scale

Spreadsheet Skills: Entering data
Entering a given formula
Inserting, deleting rows and columns
Placing headings

Materials: Spreadsheet package
Atlas (or map) indicating distance in kilometers
Ruler
Date disk

Procedure: On their spreadsheets, the students plot the path they would choose if they were traveling across the country. The headings on the worksheet, this time, would be the different cities. The students must indicate the distance between one city and the next, and run a total of the distance covered. At this stage, it will be necessary to give them the formula to add up the figures.

This activity, of course, would be easily applicable to any unit of your curriculum (Japan, Europe, the world!).

See sample worksheet on page 54. Notice the formula in the cell window.

continued...

... continued

STUDENT ACTIVITY SHEET　　　　　　**Name**_____

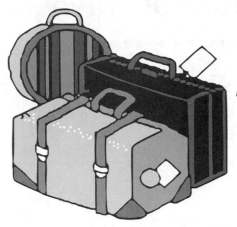

Keeping Track of Travel

CONGRATULATIONS! YOU HAVE JUST WON A FREE TRIP!

Your teacher will tell you in which part of the world, but you decide on your itinerary! So load your spreadsheet program, and BON VOYAGE!

You will need an atlas (or map) of your area, which will tell you the distance (km) between each city, or a ruler if you are going to use the scale. You will also need to know how to make the spreadsheet program add those distance figures automatically. Your teacher will tell you how to do that!

1.　Enter your first city (point of departure), then your second.

2.　You must now enter the distance (km) between the two.

3.　Now the third city. When you have entered it, enter the distance between that and the second city, and add it to the previous total with the formula your teacher gave you. The idea is to keep a running total of the distance traveled. Your teacher will show you an example.

Questions:

• How far did you travel in all?

　_____ km

• What is the distance between your first city and your third city?

　_____ km

• What is the distance between your first city and your fifth city?

　_____ km

• What is the distance between your second city and your third city?

　_____ km

• What is the distance between your fourth city and your fifth city?

　_____ km

continued...

... **continued**

Keeping Track of Travel

 File   Edit   Formula   Format   Data   Options   Macro   Window

| C12 | | =SUM(B8:B12) |

Travel log – SS

	A	B	C	D	E
1		MY TRAVEL LOG - EUROPE			
2					
3		DIFFERENCE	TOTAL		
4		BETWEEN	DISTANCE		
5		TWO CITIES			
6	CITY	In km			
7					
8	DUBLIN, IRELAND	0	0		
9	LONDON, ENGLAND	500	500		
10	PARIS, FRANCE	350	850		
11	MADRID, SPAIN	1100	1950		
12	LISBON, PORTUGAL	400	2350		
13	ROME, ITALY	2000	4350		
14	GENEVA, SWITZERLAND	760	5110		
15	AMSTERDAM, NETHERLANDS	1600	6710		
16	BERLIN, GERMANY	1200	7910		
17	BUDAPEST, HUNGARY	750	8660		
18	ATHENS, GREECE	1180	9840		
19					

Reprinted with the permission of Sonja Karsh

■ The real power of spreadsheets lies in the way students can ask "what if" questions. By simply changing an entry in the spreadsheet, it is possible to see the effect of that change on the system as a whole. This "what if" question serves two purposes — it lets students explore the system represented by the spreadsheet, and it also lets them make and test their own hypotheses.[5]

Spreadsheets are more than simply rows and columns of numbers. They "can be a valuable tool in science, mathematics and social studies by developing and reinforcing skills in problem solving, generalizing, predicting, decision making and hypothesizing."[6] Spreadsheets are useful for keeping budgets for milk and juice sales, hot dog days, bake sales, or other fund-raisers. These are great class projects when the students are in charge of the budget! All students can be involved in the creation of the spreadsheet template and different teams can be assigned responsibilities such as advertising, sales, inventory, and record-keeping. The illustrations on the preceding pages are some other examples of how the use of spreadsheets can enhance the curriculum.

CD-ROM learning materials

Educational materials in CD-ROM format are rapidly gaining popularity: they last for years, allow students to rapidly access large quantities of information, and are dropping in price. You can choose from a variety of encyclopedias and atlases. Speak to colleagues who are using an encyclopedia on CD-ROM with their students, ask sales representatives to give demonstrations, and read reviews by educators. When comparison shopping for a multimedia encyclopedia, consider the following:

- How does the price compare to others?
- Is it compatible with your hardware?
- How easy is it to install?
- Are there easy-to-access help screens, relatively free of technological jargon?
- Is there a tutorial?
- Does the menu provide a variety of entry paths for students to follow when researching?
- Is the screen display attractive and easily readable (color, print size, use of graphics)?
- Does it have a built-in dictionary/glossary?
- Does it have a notebook in which students can make and print notes?
- Can the user insert bookmarks in order to return to specific points?
- If it has sound, is the quality acceptable and for what purpose(s) is the sound used?
- How good is the quality of the still pictures, video, and animation?
- Does it include an atlas? (You may prefer to buy a separate atlas for better quality and more flexibility.)

Books in CD-ROM format are available for all ages and the selection is increasing. These "talking books," as they are often called, are especially beneficial to beginning readers, reluctant readers, and students learning English as a second language. Price determines the number of special features obtained in these on-screen books. Sound, animation, and special effects bring words to life for children and make CD-ROM books highly motivating. Highlighted words are pronounced and defined when the reader selects them. Many of these books require a sound board in the computer. Headphones are needed for an individual student and external speakers are needed if two or more students are to listen simultaneously.

Multimedia

With multimedia, students can create their own "talking books"! There are a variety of definitions of multimedia but all seem to agree that it is a combination of two or more media and all assume interactivity through the computer. Thus, interactive multimedia refers to a system that allows students to access, control, and organize information in a variety of ways, using graphics, text, animation, video, and audio. It provides links that connect facts, ideas, words, and pictures.

Picture the traditional student research project, consisting of text and pictures on a large sheet of cardboard or in a folder, transformed into a computer-driven presentation of text, still and/or moving images, and sound. Multimedia is very appealing to students because it allows them to organize and present information using the same media through which they are used to receiving it. They become active participants rather than merely passive recipients of information.

Multimedia is still too new to have been thoroughly tested and researched in classrooms, but early feedback is most encouraging. Isabelle Bruder[7] maintains that multimedia is superior to more traditional classroom tools because it:

- reaches all of the senses and can be tailored to meet the learning styles of different learners;
- encourages self-expression;
- gives a sense of ownership to the user;
- creates an active rather than passive learning environment;
- fosters communication, student to student and student to teacher;
- makes sense because technology is already built into the lives of students;
- is a lot of fun.

■ It [multimedia] gives students "hands-on" learning, better retention, specific feedback, and increased levels of understanding. We can't consistently make these statements about videotape, text, text with graphics, traditional classroom learning or even computer-based training.[8]

A multimedia workstation, in its simplest form, might consist of a computer, VCR, TV, video camera, and videodisc player. The computer is the hub and the additional equipment serves as the multimedia peripherals. By combining these technologies in various ways, students can do multimedia research, prepare reports, and make presentations to an audience.

A high-end, sophisticated multimedia workstation could cost $10 000 or more. Think of it as a computer system capable of capturing, storing, producing, and transmitting multimedia documents. These documents could contain words, numbers, sound, moving and still images, and three-dimensional models. A system with this degree of sophistication is likely to be a school-wide, shared resource rather than a classroom resource. It could be placed on a cart and moved around to act as a mobile audiovisual studio or publishing center. As prices fall, use of this type of system will probably become more widespread.

The term multimedia platform is often used to describe the computer software that allows the integration of various types of media into one document. The variety of platforms available today enables children as young as six or seven to create simple multimedia presentations and senior students to produce products of professional quality. Some platforms use a system of index cards through which the user links information. Others use a flowchart or branching technique. Regardless of the method, students must apply skills in language, research, organization, sequencing, graphic design, logic, and creativity to program their own presentations.

A minimal amount of equipment can serve a class when students work in teams or cooperative learning groups. Individual students on the team could become experts in different areas such as scriptwriting, filming, researching, and publishing.

When beginning multimedia work, provide time for teams to experiment, improvise, and innovate. The additional time required to produce a multimedia project as opposed to a traditional project is worthwhile when you consider the skills that students develop in the process.

■ The new media can be more than a spectator sport for millions of virtual-reality armchair voyeurs and jocks. It's going to be cheap, fast, and easy to use — for adults and kindergartners alike. And it doesn't have to be crafted by the likes of Lucas, Spielberg, and Schwartzenegger. It can be created by toddlers, teens, teachers — by you and me. The new media can be more than an electronic spectacle. It's an opportunity for all of us to be artists, musicians, sculptors, composers — and readers and writers![9]

Teachers who are most successful with multimedia introduce it in a learning environment that includes cooperative learning, higher-order thinking skills, risk-taking, group problem solving, and students taking responsibility for their own learning. Some training in using multimedia technology is required, so if this brief glimpse arouses your interest in exploring and using multimedia, look for user groups, workshops, and courses in your local area.

■ It is best to follow the "K-I-S-S" rule of multimedia, especially when you are just getting started:

Keep It Simple to Get Started!
Keep It Short and Sweet!
Keep It Simple to Survive![10]

Figure 4.1

This sample screen illustrates one way in which a student might use authoring software to program a simple multimedia project about Canada. In the center is a flowchart that sequences the various elements of the presentation. At the side are some of the options and different media that can be used.

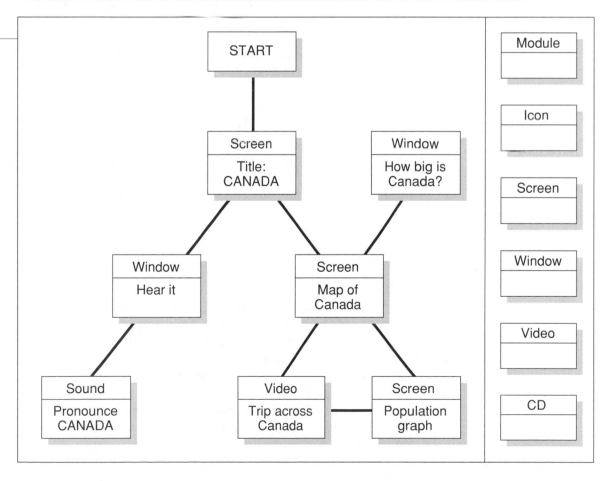

Telecommunications

In its simplest form, telecommunications means communicating across distance using the tools of computers, modems, and telephone lines. Telecommunications allows teachers and students to electronically explore the world without ever leaving the classroom. Researching information, conferencing with other computer users who share your interests, and sending and receiving electronic mail are but a few of the activities available. We can provide only an overview in this brief section and thus refer you to books specifically on this subject for further information.[11]

■ As more telecommunications projects are developed, there will be a continual move away from didactic learning to collaborative learning and the nurturing of thinking skills for exploring a multi-faceted curriculum. The use of educational telecommunications is now at the forefront of technology education. Educators are now dealing with the reality of having to teach students this new technology. This process will require teachers to again, as with the teaching of computer literacy, develop and deliver materials, hardware and software to integrate telecommunications across the curriculum.[12]

The following are some of the reasons why telecommunications, or "going on-line," is becoming so popular as a teaching and learning tool:

- Telecommunications provides students with a meaningful context in which to master skills.[13]
- It provides a broad base of data not normally available in one location, such as on-line systems, central databanks, electronic bulletin boards, and direct communication with individuals in different geographic locations. It opens up the world for students!
- It provides additional sources of ideas: teachers, students, and experts.
- It allows users to directly exchange datafiles such as personally produced documents and public domain programs.
- It provides a real and diverse audience.[14] This audience outside the classroom has a motivational effect on students.[15]
- It eliminates visible characteristics such as age, race, social position, and handicaps.
- It allows the parties to communicate at convenient times.
- It enhances inquiry and analytical skills.
- It overcomes two common classroom problems: isolation and lack of up-to-date information.

Telecommunications requires specific software, and many computers come with a suitable software package. A wide variety of software is also available for purchase. Such software is called communications software, modem software, or possibly terminal emulation software. Some packages are specific to one brand of computer, while others are sold in different versions for different machines. Packages vary in complexity. As always, the kind of software you need is determined by what you want to do. User-friendliness is an important criterion for beginners and younger students. You do not need to have the same software as the host (the computer with which you want to communicate).

Once you have the hardware, software, and telephone line in place, you need to find out how to access an electronic database, computer communications service, and/or an electronic bulletin board. Some of these are free but most have an annual or monthly fee. Subscription fees include documentation, some on-line time, and sometimes classroom curricular materials. This kind of information is location-specific and constantly changing, so you need to thoroughly explore the services and information available in your community before selecting and planning a telecommunications project. Some of the features you might look for include:

- electronic mail;
- conferencing;
- curriculum projects;
- access to higher education networks and services;

- access to experts;
- bulletin boards;
- on-line tutoring;
- access to a variety of databases;
- access to other networks.

When embarking on telecommunications with your students, start with a small project.[16] Introduce your students to the concept of telecommunications through diagrams or role-playing activities.

■ I feel sorry for my parents having to use handwriting or manual typewriters to do their essays and projects, and especially sorry that the only way they could communicate abroad until now was by either mail or telephone. It's good to see that they will at least get to experience what I am experiencing for some of their life. (Duncan Clark, 16 [17])

Figure 4.2

When students understand the series of events that allows for telecommunications to occur, they are better able to manipulate the components.

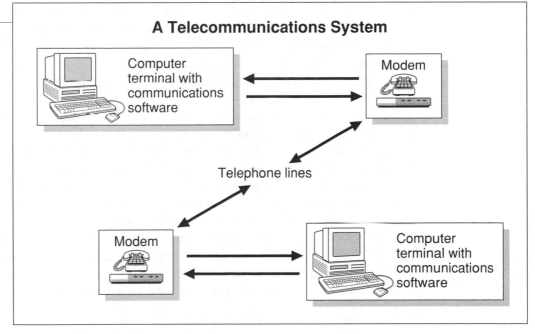

A Telecommunications System

Computer terminal with communications software

Modem

Telephone lines

Modem

Computer terminal with communications software

Proceed slowly, always keeping in mind the educational objectives. Do not introduce computer networking as an add-on — integrate it into your curriculum. A good way to introduce students to the concept of communicating through the computer is to develop language skills using a "chat" program; that is, a technique where one computer is connected to another so that students can communicate via their computers by keying messages back and forth. If your school has a LAN (local area network), you will have no difficulty finding chat software and making connections within and/or between classrooms. It is like chatting on the telephone, except that students must use their speaking and listening skills in the form of reading and writing. Not only is language development promoted because it occurs in a meaningful context, but these interactive programs are highly motivating and lend themselves to cooperative learning and group problem solving. Editing skills are also enhanced by the immediate feedback and peer editing becomes natural. Activities for chat programs might include cooperative story writing, discussion of current issues or news events, and "who is" or "what is" games in which students use their questioning skills to determine the identity of a mystery person or thing.

Once you move on from chatting to accessing commercially established and government-sponsored networks, you will find quite a range of possibilities. The following sample activities are appropriate for beginners and illustrate the wide variety of experiences available through telecommunications:

- Have students share their writing with established authors through an electronic writers-in-residence program. The authors become mentors and coaches to assist the students in refining their writing skills.
- Link students with peers in another country or part of the country. Through ongoing dialogue, they learn about demographics, climate, and cultural similarities and differences.
- Collaborate with another teacher in order to assign a common project to students in two different locations. A problem-solving exercise or mystery/detective game lends itself well. Establish cooperative learning groups that include members from each location and assist students in sharing ideas and work.
- Create a scavenger hunt by hiding messages for students on an electronic bulletin board. Each message might lead them to another location on the network. This way, students will learn to explore the various subdirectories.
- Pair students with a telecommunications pal in another school. Have the pals communicate during the year, providing some structure for their on-line discussions. Plan a year-end event at which the pals meet in person.
- Have students select a question to answer, problem to solve, or topic to research, using the many resources available on the network.
- Contact a scientist at a university or museum who can answer students' questions on-line relevant to a science topic they are studying.
- Join a science group that collects and shares data on an environmental issue. National Geographic Kids Network is an existing network that uses this technique. One example is a project in which students examine acid rain, under the supervision of an experienced scientist. Students form part of a team with other schools to collect scientific data. They send their data in to a central databank and receive maps of the country showing trends in acid rain, which they are then asked to explain. Thus, the students act as real scientists.

■ Our teachers tell us that we will be able to tell our kids that we were the first to communicate with other classrooms around the world without leaving our desks. This is more than just a school project, it's a sign of hope. What else can you call an exchange of ideas between three different countries and six different states? (Scott Wilson, 17 [18])

More sophisticated projects are likely to emerge naturally once students, who have been familiar with telecommunications in their personal lives for several generations already, embrace telecommunications as an element of their learning environment. Encourage student-initiated projects as they become comfortable using telecommunications independently. Set time-lines for the completion of activities[19] so that they do not drag on for too long. Although it can be difficult to access the network at the specific time that you want, try to involve the students in the sending and receiving of messages in order to stimulate their interest and familiarity with telecommunications.[20] Depending on the popularity of the network you are using, messages may have to be collected and sent after hours.

Videotapes and videodiscs

The use of videotapes and videodiscs maintains student interest, promotes visual literacy, and increases acquisition of knowledge.[21] We have put these two into one category because the evaluation criteria in terms of quality and content are similar, but there are more factors to think about when buying and using a videodisc than a videotape. The big difference between VCR video and computer video is interactivity: instead of sitting and viewing, in linear fashion, a presentation created by someone else, computer video allows students to "do" — to exert control over the creation and/or viewing. A videodisc is a visual database. Using a videodisc, you can easily sift through the visual materials in any order and at any speed you want.

A quick look at a videodisc catalog reveals two kinds of discs. The CLV (continuous linear velocity) disc stores up to 60 minutes of material per side, which can be accessed by time codes or chapter numbers. The CAV (continuous angular velocity) disc is more flexible, permitting chapter searches, frame searches, and single-frame stepping and scanning with a running time of 30 minutes. The relative price of CLV versus CAV reflects the difference in flexibility of use. Some videodiscs, however, are simply videotapes put onto disc and may have little advantage for the extra price. Think of the videodisc not as merely the modern replacement for the videotape, but rather as a tool that allows greater quality, flexibility, motivation, interactivity, individualization, and student control. Students and teachers who *use* video instead of just *showing* it, greatly increase its value as an educational tool.

■ Don't forget about TV — it can educate as well as entertain! Look for TV programs that address appropriate content and skills, fit your available time frame, are flexible, and are of good quality. Many networks offer curriculum guides jam-packed with ideas. Consider ways of using newscasts, documentaries, dramas, sports events, weather reports, bulletin boards, and commercials, as well as instructional programming.

Be sure to preview videotapes and videodiscs before selecting them for classroom use, with these questions in mind:

• How well does the content fit the curriculum you are teaching?
• What can students *do* with the content presented?
• Is the vocabulary age appropriate for students?
• Is the program true to life in its portrayal of characters?
• Is the narrative powerful and meaningful?

- Is there variety in presentation of content?
- Is it free of bias and are minorities represented?
- Is the quality of audio and video excellent? (The resolution of a videodisc should be better than that of a videotape.)
- Is the videodisc divided into sections or chapters so that students can easily access specific parts?
- Does it have a teacher guidebook? (A guidebook can help you locate information quickly and may also contain suggestions for activities.)
- Do bar codes accompany the videodisc?

Resources are available that list hundreds of different titles.[22] Many titles are in the science and computer areas, but recently the strongest areas of growth are art, language arts, and social studies titles.[23]

■ Consider this quote: "The age of illustration is upon us and illustrate we must if we hope to gain the attention of young and old." When was it written? Go ahead, take a guess. . . . Of course, these 19th century quotes refer to the magic lantern. For those of you who don't still have the magic lanterns in your school, the device resembled an early slide projector, except the slides were big and made of glass and the light source came from flame. The magic lantern could display a big picture on a blank wall, so you can see why this equipment was highly touted. In the mid to late 1800s, some educational reformers complained that there was just too much teacher talk in the classroom. That's just *not* how kids, or adults for that matter, learned.[24]

CHAPTER 5

What About Curriculum?

Over a five-year period, the Education Development Center (EDC) carried out a two-phased project to better understand how teachers can successfully integrate technology into the middle school curriculum. . . . One finding that clearly emerged from this study was that successful technology integration should start with a strong, effective curriculum that meets the intellectual, social and physical needs of young adolescents.[1]

Assume that you have decided to plan a unit in which technology is an integral component. You want to use technology to enhance your child-centered classroom, to assist in teaching and learning, to motivate and excite students. Whichever subject(s) you choose, you will find that the steps to successful planning of a technology-integrated unit are similar to planning any unit of study — logical and straightforward. We recommend an eight-step process, as shown in Figure 5.1 on the next page. In each step, consider the possible advantages that technology has to offer.

Step 1: Select a topic

If your choice of topics is controlled by curriculum set in place by your school or school system, there are probably guidelines as to the depth and breadth of content and the expected learning outcomes for students in terms of knowledge, skills, and attitudes. There may be benchmarks or mastery skills that students must strive to reach through your carefully planned activities. However, if you do have free choice of topics, consider that topics may stem from a wide variety of places and experiences. Some possible sources are:

- an experience that one or several students have had;
- an artifact brought in by you or a student that excites interest;
- a story, article, or idea that you have seen and researched;
- a particular interest of yours;
- an incident from the news or some everyday event that has had an impact on the students or sparked a particular interest;
- a closer look at some familiar object that we tend to take for granted;
- a library book or a favorite story;
- an area of expertise of a particular student.

Figure 5.1

These curriculum planning steps can be used to create a successful technology-integrated unit. The dotted lines illustrate that the steps are interrelated and interdependent.

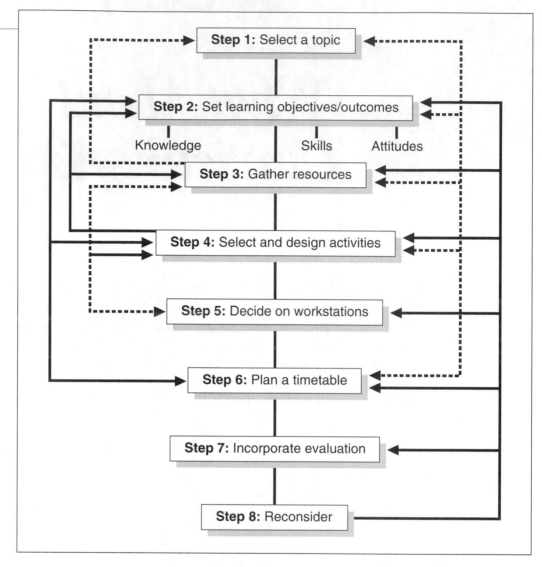

Brainstorming the topic with colleagues and students results in the consideration of related ideas and concepts. Motivation and interest are also enhanced when students are involved in planning. Ideas can be grouped on a flowchart or list, as shown in Figure 5.2. Your goal of enhanced inclusion of technology will already be apparent in this first step of planning.

Step 2: Establish learning objectives/outcomes

Become familiar with the knowledge, skills, and attitudes that students are expected to develop through the study of the selected topic. Whether you select these learning objectives/outcomes or they are designated by the central core curriculum of the school or school system, keep them in mind as you proceed through the planning process. They are your guide for students' process and products and the focus for evaluation. You may wish to establish some learning objectives/outcomes related specifically to the technology that students will be using; for example:

- accessing information through a telecommunications network;
- organizing data on a spreadsheet;
- preparing a multimedia presentation;
- using a simple word processor to produce a product;
- integrating graphics with text;
- producing a video.

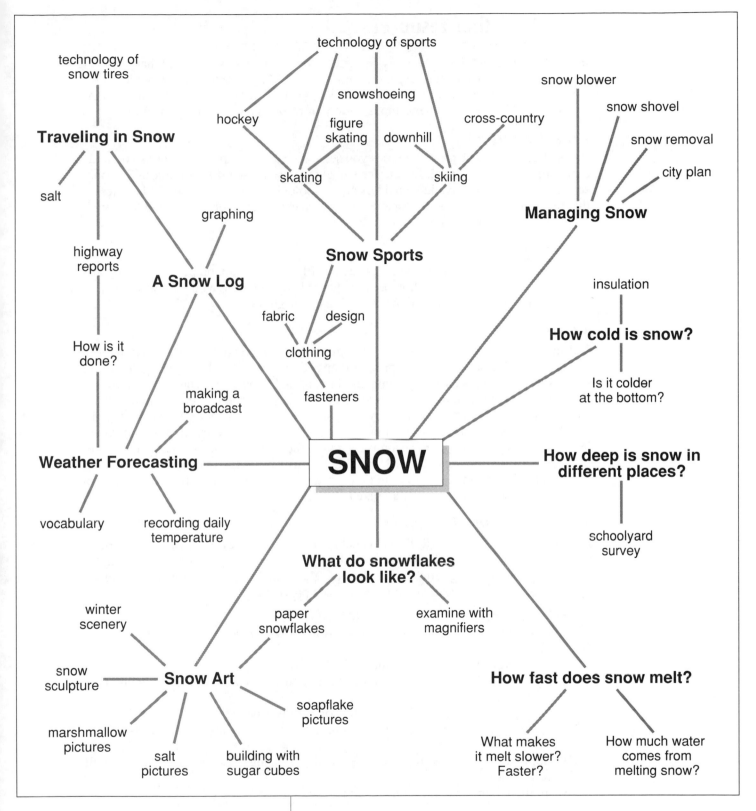

Figure 5.2

This flowchart, created in a classroom of 9- to 12-year-olds, illustrates the inclusion of technological concepts in a unit about snow. The many subtopics provide a framework for the development of activities in which students use technology to access, organize, and communicate information.

Step 3: Gather resources

In the development of a technology-integrated unit, teachers usually find that gathering resources challenges them to expand their horizons. When we think of resources, we tend to think of various print resources and videos, but thanks to the advancements of technology, there is now an enormous variety of resources from which to choose.

Print Resources

Regardless of the non-print resources you select, a classroom library of books related to the topic is still essential. Encourage students to use these print resources. Plan on searching through the available readers and anthologies in the school to find stories that relate to the topic. Use newspaper and magazine articles for variety and to provide more current information for your students.

Audiotapes

Do not ignore older existing resources such as filmstrips or audiotapes unless they are hopelessly outdated. If no audiotapes are available on the topic, you may wish to record some appropriate selections, honoring copyright laws.

Videotapes

Videotapes can usually be borrowed through a central media outlet. Educational TV channels provide some excellent programming. Check your local program guide to see if any shows or series currently being aired relate to the topic that you have chosen. The time that a particular program is aired on TV may make it difficult or impossible to integrate it into your timetable; however, some television broadcasts may be taped for classroom showing at a more appropriate time. Again, be aware of copyright laws. When selecting videotapes to accompany a unit, the length of the tape may determine its classroom use. For example, a 45-minute segment is best for whole-group viewing, whereas a 15- to 20-minute program or a shorter clip is more useful for small-group or individual viewing, followed by a related activity.

Videodiscs and CD-ROMs

If a videodisc and/or a CD-ROM is available on the topic, preview it carefully in order to determine its best use. These resources have a great deal of potential for student motivation and learning. You may wish to use the same item several times in different ways. The following questions can be used as a previewing guide:

- Is it appropriate for the targeted age group?
- Does it include specific content or skills that I want students to master in this unit?
- What part or parts do I want the students to view?
- Is it best used as a student resource/research tool or would it best be included as part of a lesson?
- Are there specific points at which to stop for discussion?
- Does it lend itself better to whole-group discussion? Small-group discussion? Individual reflection?
- Should a follow-up activity be based on this viewing? If so, whole-group? Small group? Individual?
- Are there helpful suggestions in the teacher's guide?

An encyclopedia on CD-ROM may be available in a technology-integrated classroom or school resource center. It is difficult to imagine a unit in which this resource would *not* be useful. The challenge is to design student activities that incorporate the use of this technology to achieve specific learning outcomes for your students.

Computers

In compiling resources for a unit, explore the applications of classroom computers. Here, you are limited only by your imagination and the available software! Consider the following issues when deciding on how to use computers in the study of a specific topic:

- How can students best use a word processor in this unit:
  - writing notes?
  - creative writing?
  - research reports?
  - letter-writing?
  - other?
- Is student use of a database appropriate in this unit?
- Is a ready-made database available that relates to this topic?
- Would student creation of a database assist in the development of the selected knowledge, skills, or attitudes of this unit?
- Would a spreadsheet be useful for any activity that students might pursue, either individually or as a group?
- Would a graphics program provide another way to learn skills, reinforce knowledge, and/or present findings?
- Is any other software available that relates to this topic:
  - simulation?
  - programming and/or control technologies?
  - drill and practice?
  - other?
- Can telecommunications be used to obtain information related to this topic?
- Can an electronic bulletin board be used to allow students to communicate with other students studying the same topic?
- How can students enhance their presentation of products by using the computer?

■ Just as teachers plan subject areas, so should some time be devoted to planning for classroom computing. . . . Using the computer in a haphazard manner or on the spur of the moment often results in many classroom disruptions and few educational benefits.[2]

Concrete materials

Do not overlook the simple but valuable hands-on materials such as hammers, pulleys, tangrams, and the many other manipulatives so useful in an active learning environment. The term active learning reflects a particular belief in the way that children learn — by actively investigating the world that surrounds them, by interacting with people, and by manipulating concrete materials. An active learning program provides the child with opportunities to explore materials, ideas, and relationships. Although technology is engaging for children, it should not take the place of the real experience. Watching a video of life in the forest may give the student a feeling for it, but it is not equivalent to being there. For the young student, moving numbers around on a computer screen to make a $3 + 5 = 8$ number sentence may be useful at the semi-abstract level, but it does not replace the concrete experience of counting out blocks.

■ We learn . . .

10% of what we read	70% of what is discussed with others
20% of what we hear	80% of what we experience personally
30% of what we see	90% of what we teach to someone else[3]
50% of what we both see and hear	

Community resources

Your community can provide wonderful resources, such as places to visit (e.g., museums, businesses, and manufacturing industries) and people who will come into your classroom to share specialized knowledge and interests. You can often access these resources through a telecommunications network. Teachers have often been surprised to see the community resources that show up when a "parent letter" is sent home announcing the beginning of a new and exciting unit of study!

Step 4: Select and design activities

With student learning objectives, the flowchart of the topic, and the list of resources that you have collected and researched, you are well prepared to begin the challenging task of creating activities for students. In designing activities, try to maximize the use of all of the technology available.

Figure 5.3

Balance whole-group involvement, small-group activities, and individual pursuits and include both teacher-directed and student-centered activities. Figure 5.5 on page 75 provides a sample daily plan for a measurement unit.

■ In her studies of teaching and learning at the Education Development Centre in Massachusetts, Judith Zorfass found that "Technology use was most successful when teachers brought technology into curriculum contexts where students were actively engaged in pursuing authentic tasks in which they were invested, and where teachers facilitated the learning process by guiding and coaching their students. Within the context of a strong curriculum, technology had the potential of enhancing teaching and learning."[4]

Resource books, teachers' manuals, the guides that accompany audiovisual materials, workshop handouts, education courses, etc., can all trigger the creation of exciting and educationally sound activities. Opportunities for the students themselves to make choices and pursue investigations of subtopics and issues in which they are interested will enhance motivation and learning.

Planning a Measurement Unit		
Whole-Group Activities	**Small-Group Activities**	**Individual Activities**
Review measurement vocabulary.	Estimate perimeters and check.	At workstations:
Measure student's height and weight.	Estimate areas and check.	Review addition and multiplication of three-digit numbers.
View videos: perimeter, area, volume, capacity, and mass.	Draw polygons and find area.	Listening tapes to practice selecting appropriate units.
Calculate perimeter and area (m, dm, cm).	Make buildings from centicubes.	Concrete activities in each type of measurement.
Measure volume using centicubes.	Measure capacity in L and mL.	Computer: Program for practice in measurement.
Make a cubic meter.	Measure mass in g and kg.	Problem solving involving each type of measurement.
Temperature chart for the month.	Make daily time schedules.	View videos a second time and do follow-up activity.

Figure 5.4

There are many different formats for organizing student activities. This approach uses a Venn diagram.

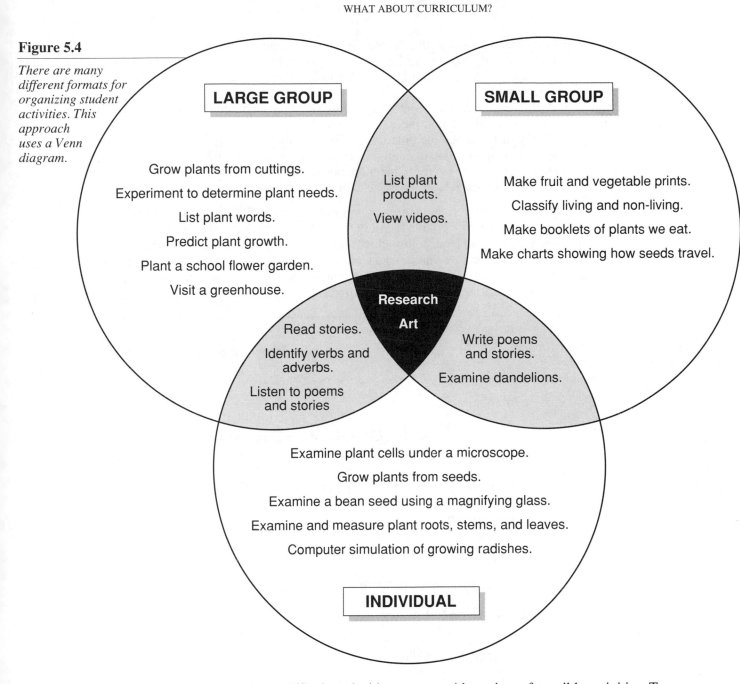

It is sometimes difficult to decide among a wide variety of possible activities. Try asking these questions when selecting and designing activities:

- Does this activity focus on specific knowledge, skills, or attitudes that I want students to develop, master, or review in this unit?
- Do I have, or can I easily obtain, the materials required for students to complete this activity?
- Do I have the space to store these materials and for students to work with them?
- How long will it take students to complete this activity?
- Do I have enough time to include this activity?
- Are most or all of the students in my class capable of completing this activity?
- Can the students read the directions?
- Can the students follow the directions?
- Do the students have the prerequisite skills required?
- Can the activity be easily modified for exceptional students?

- Can students work with a partner or have the support of a group?
- Is this activity too easy or basic for the more advanced students in my class?
- Is it open-ended or can it be modified to suit more advanced students' needs for enrichment?
- Will students have access to the resources and/or technology required at the time that they need it to complete this activity?
- How will I evaluate the outcome of this activity?
- Is it more appropriate to evaluate process, product, or both?
- How well will this activity meet the perceived needs and interests of the students as they were expressed when we explored the topic together?

An activity card format is often appropriate for individual assignments and sometimes also for cooperative learning tasks. To successfully work from an activity card, students need to read; follow directions; organize appropriate materials, resources, and work areas; and make some decisions on their own. If your students are used to a more teacher-directed approach, spend some extra time practicing these skills before requiring independent work from activity cards.

This activity card for a younger student, taken from a unit about fairy tales and fables, requires the student to listen to a story on audiotape and follow up with a brief written assignment.

Center: Speaking/Listening
Card: 4AA

The Hidden Treasure

Listen to the story "The Treasure in the Orchard."

Finish each sentence.

1. The treasure was _____

2. The son's smooth hands got _____

3. Next year, the brothers will _____

(rough and dirty.)

(work hard in the orchard.)

(the oranges, apples, and cherries.)

Instructional skill: Predicting

Inquiry/Thinking skill: Critical Thinking: Comprehension

Learning strategy: Listening, Reporting

Materials: paper, pencil, tape: "The Treasure in the Orchard"

Activity type: small group
individual **X**

Reprinted with the permission of the Carleton Roman Catholic School Board

The sample activity cards shown on these pages are written at various levels of difficulty. They are not intended to represent the ideal nor all of the possible types of activities, but rather to illustrate how student use of technology can be integrated with skill development on an activity card.

> ■ Four boys were overheard while working on an assignment based on a video. They reached the last question: "Would you like a challenge? Try the Think Tank question." One student said, "Let's try it." Another said, "We don't *have* to do that question." A third said, "It'll be fun!" They decided to do it.

This activity comes from a unit about microscopy at the 9- to 10-year-old level.

Center: Writing
Card: 6C

Take Care

Write a paragraph that explains, in detail, how a detective might use a microscope to solve a crime.

You may want to use a word processing program

> **Remember:** topic sentence
> developing sentences
> closing sentence

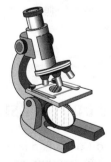

Instructional skill: Paragraph Formation, Creative Writing

Inquiry/Thinking skill: Critical Thinking: Synthesis
  Creative Thinking: Flexibility, Originality

Learning strategy: Storymaking and Editing

Materials: paper, pencil, or word
  processing program

Activity type: small group
  individual **X**

After having completed whole-group and small-group concrete experiences with angle creation and measurement, the student is directed to use Logo procedures on the computer to practice identifying types of triangles. Each procedure (tri1, tri2, etc.) creates a triangle for the student to analyze. This activity was created for 11- to 12-year-old students.

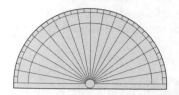

Center: Math Problem Solving
Card: 2C

Triangle Types

Login under one of the special logins from logo1 to logo16
Type - *load "toolkit.* Press Enter.

Copy the following chart in your notebook. Use each of the procedures on the chart to create a triangle and use your ruler and protractor to complete the chart.

Remember: After each triangle, beside the ? type *cs* and press Enter to clear the screen.

Procedure	# of Equal Sides	# of Equal Angles	Type of Triangle
tri1			
tri2			
tri4			
tri5			
tri6			

Instructional skill: 2-D Geometric Shapes: Types of Triangles

Inquiry/Thinking skill: Critical Thinking: Application

Learning strategy: Reporting, Charting

Materials: "Logo Toolkit," protractor, paper, pencil, ruler

Activity type: small group
individual **X**

Reprinted with the permission of the Carleton Roman Catholic School Board

Step 5: Decide on workstations

Using a workstation approach is one of the best ways to ensure maximum use of the available technology. Most equipment in a technological classroom is designed for individual, partner, or small-group work. Workstations should:

- easily fit into the room;
- take into account the stages of development of individuals in the class;
- lend themselves to the extension of skills;
- incorporate all of the resources available.

Several resources are available to the 13- to 15-year-old student in this activity. Students enjoy and benefit from the option of choosing the technologies that they want to use.

Center: Research
Card: 1

Pollution from Energy Sources

Purpose: To research the causes of the greenhouse effect and the ways that we can reduce it.
To produce a poster or ad campaign to help reduce the problem.

Method: **A.** Use the electronic encyclopedia and the pamphlet *Energy and the Environment* as well as the excerpt from the *Atlas of the Environment* to find the following:

1. the causes of the greenhouse effect and the global effects of the problem, and

2. the ways that we can help reduce the problem.

B. Decide how you will present your topic as a poster or as an ad campaign. You might use a graphics program or prepare a multimedia presentation.

See your teacher to discuss your presentation.

You will be evaluated.

Content	1 2 3 4 5
Attractiveness	1 2 3 4 5
Originality	1 2 3 4 5
Presentation	1 2 3 4 5

Reprinted with the permission of the Carleton Roman Catholic School Board

The choice of workstations will, of course, depend on the age of your students, the topic, the resources available, and the activities your plan includes. Thus, workstations will vary from unit to unit. Some common workstations include:

- Arts
- Blocks
- Career awareness
- Concrete/experimental
- Drama
- Invention
- Mapping
- Mathematics
- Nature
- Problem solving
- Puppetry
- Reading
- Related skills
- Research
- Sand
- Speaking and listening
- Spelling
- Structures
- Take-apart
- Viewing
- Water
- Writing/publishing

Center: Small Group (Viewing)

Card: 3

Showing the Natural Balance

View the video "The Natural Balance."

Each group member creates a simple stick puppet to represent one level of the ecosystem (example: plant, herbivore, carnivore, omnivore, decomposer).

When all of the puppets are ready, join together to produce a short play that explains the natural balance.

Instructional skill: Content, Puppets, Drama

Inquiry/Thinking skill: Critical Thinking: Application, Synthesis

Learning strategy: Viewing & Analyzing

Materials: video "The Natural Balance," assorted art materials

Activity type: small group **X** individual

Reprinted with the permission of the Carleton Roman Catholic School Board

You will notice that the list of workstations on page 73 does not include one called "Computer" or "CD-ROM." In our concept of the technological classroom, technology is used as a tool for the accomplishment of specific activities; thus, students move to a computer, VCR, videodisc player, camera, or tape recorder as required. Chapter 6, "Getting Started," provides more detailed suggestions for organizing the classroom, materials, and routines for workstations.

Step 6: Plan a timetable

The next step is to sequence the selected activities to suit the available instruction time and to provide logical concept development. Some teachers prefer to spend a longer amount of time working with the whole group before moving into cooperative learning groups and individual pursuits. If you are just beginning the transition to a more student-centered approach that accommodates the integration of technology, this may be a good way to begin. If you are experienced in using a variety of teaching and learning styles, you may choose to provide this variety within a day, and from day to day.

When students are using technology, strict time-lines are more difficult to establish. Unforeseen events such as lack of access to a particular technology exactly when required, technical problems, and time required to become proficient with software create a need for flexibility of time allotments.

Figure 5.5

Laying out a unit on a day-to-day basis helps to establish and maintain time-lines. This example shows a more detailed plan than does Figure 5.3 and illustrates an ideal way to vary whole-group, co-operative learning, and individual work at workstations within a unit.

Sample Daily Plan for a Measurement Unit			
Day	**Activity**	**Type of Activity**	**Technology**
Monday	Review measurement vocabulary Review addition and multiplication	Whole group Individual	Overhead
Tuesday	Measure students' height and graph	 Whole group	
Wednesday	View videotape on perimeter Estimate perimeters of objects and check by measuring	Whole group Small groups	Videotape
Thursday	Workstations: perimeter	Individual	Computers, videotapes, audiotapes
Friday	Workstations: perimeter	Individual	Computers, videotapes, audiotapes
Monday	View videotape on area Estimate areas of objects and check by measuring	Whole group Small groups	Videotape
Tuesday	Draw polygons and exchange to calculate area	 Small groups	
Wednesday	Workstations: perimeter and area	Individual	Computers, videotapes, audiotapes
Thursday	Workstations: perimeter and area	Individual	Computers, videotapes, audiotapes
Friday	View videotape on volume Use centicubes to make objects with given volume	Whole group Individual	Videotape
Monday	Build a cubic meter Make buildings from centicubes and find volume	Whole group Small groups	

Tuesday	Workstations: perimeter, area,
	  and volume
		
		Individual
			Computers, videotapes,
			  audiotapes

Wednesday	Workstations: perimeter, area,
	  and volume
		
		Individual
			Computers, videotapes,
			  audiotapes

Thursday	Workstations: perimeter, area,
	  and volume
		
		Individual
			Computers, videotapes,
			  audiotapes

Friday	View videotape on capacity Measure in L and mL	Whole group Small groups	Videotape

Monday	Workstations: perimeter, area,
	  volume, and capacity
		
		Individual
			Computers, videotapes,
			  audiotapes, CD-ROM

Tuesday	Workstations: perimeter, area,
	  volume, and capacity
		
		Individual
			Computers, videotapes,
			  audiotapes, CD-ROM

Wednesday	Workstations: perimeter, area,
	  volume, and capacity
		
		Individual
			Computers, videotapes,
			  audiotapes, CD-ROM

Step 7: Incorporate evaluation

Diagnostic, formative, and summative evaluations are components of all units. The tremendous diversity of needs within any class requires individualization of programs. Technology can be of great assistance in the evaluation process. This issue is considered in greater detail in Chapter 8, "Evaluating Student Progress."

Step 8: Reconsider

Although this step-by-step approach to planning a curriculum unit may appear at first to be very linear, all of the steps are interrelated and interdependent. Cohesive planning is achieved by constantly referring back to earlier decisions. As you lay out your completed plan, stop and reconsider. Is there a sound purpose behind each workstation? Is each selected activity consistent with the learning objectives for the topic? Does your planned evaluation adequately reflect those same learning objectives? Have you achieved your goal of integrating technology into the curriculum? If you answer "Yes" to all of these questions, then you are ready to start!

CHAPTER 6

Getting Started

Innovation will require not only education reform but a reformation of our concepts of learning, working, and management. Making the experience of learning self-engaging, creating an environment for learning that is fun, and providing personal tools to make technology as transparent as possible are all necessary steps.[1]

For a classroom teacher, the opportunity exists to make technology as much a part of students' experience at school as it already is in their daily lives outside of school. Making careful and strategic decisions at the classroom level will enhance your students' performance and will streamline the implementation of your technology-integrated program. Proceed slowly. Students will not become self-motivated, self-directed, and technology-literate overnight. You are likely to find, however, that many students adapt more quickly to the use of technology than you do. Use this natural adaptability to the advantage of all by allowing these students to demonstrate the use of hardware and software to the class and encouraging them to act as resource persons for others who are less experienced. By showing that you are also a learner, you establish a positive classroom learning environment, model authentic problem-solving strategies, and move into the role of a facilitator of learning.

Call on resource people within your school and/or school system who can assist you, especially with the physical setup and operation of the classroom. Perhaps contact a consultant, another teacher, a resource teacher, or librarian who is comfortable with using technical equipment or a personal friend who is hooked on technology. The next chapter, "The Well-Mannered, Safe, Technological Classroom," provides more suggestions for the ongoing operation of your technological classroom.

Organizing space

Activity-based learning requires particular types of spaces, configurations, and easy-to-reach storage facilities and resources. However, space is often a rare commodity. Nonetheless, ingenuity on the part of teachers and students has led to well-equipped, well-designed workstations, even within the confines of a single, small classroom!

When planning the physical layout, consider the type of learning environment you want to create. An ideal environment:

- stimulates active learning;
- allows flexibility in work modes as a member of a group, with a partner, or individually;
- provides easy access to resources and equipment.

Positioning computers

The equipment that takes up the most space, usually computers, should be set up first. Positioning computers is governed by several factors:

- the location of the cable that connects the computer(s) to the school network (unless the computers all stand alone);
- the location of power outlets;
- the location of doorways leading into the classroom;
- the location of windows — too much direct light makes it difficult to see the computer screen and is also distracting;
- the location of chalkboards — chalk dust can damage computers, so some schools are substituting whiteboards.

Most classrooms have only two or three power outlets so the location options are immediately limited. However, power bars enable several computers to operate from one power outlet. Be sure to check with your local fire department and with your school or school system's safety officer regarding fire and electrical regulations. Wires should never pass across floor space where people walk, and running extension cords across doorways violates electrical codes. See Chapter 7, "The Well-Mannered, Safe, Technological Classroom," for more safety considerations.

In arranging tables for computers, several choices are possible, as illustrated in the photographs on these pages.

Positioning computers along a wall is an economical use of space. This arrangement makes it easy to observe students at work, but in some classrooms it might restrict access to bulletin boards or display space. The screens might also prove distracting to other students.

If computers are arranged in a circle, allow enough space between them for a notebook, activity card, and/or mouse pad.

If the computers are all stand-alone, rather than networked, they do not necessarily have to be grouped together and the choice of locations is limited only by the availability of power outlets. Because there will often be two chairs at each computer, allow enough space for other students to pass by without disturbing the concentration of those working on-screen. It is a good idea to position at least one computer facing into the classroom for occasions when you or a student want to demonstrate something to the whole group. A printer must be easily accessible to students and the paper should feed freely, without interference from wires or other equipment.

Placement of TV/VCR

Once you have set up the computers, you can then arrange the other equipment requiring power outlets. A TV/VCR is susceptible to interference from bright sunlight and is thus best positioned in a corner where students can gather around for viewing. If the primary use of the TV/VCR is individual or small-group viewing, invite younger students to sit on a carpet.

The shape of the computer tables sometimes inspires a different arrangement. A combination of rectangular and trapezoidal tables has been used here for economy of space.

Older students may prefer to pull their chairs closely around the TV/VCR so that individual headphones can reach it. Five or six sets of headphones reserved for use at the TV/VCR will usually suffice in a class of 30 students. Encourage students to help in getting organized. One student could be in charge of operating the equipment.

Students may want to sit at a desk or table so they can write while viewing.

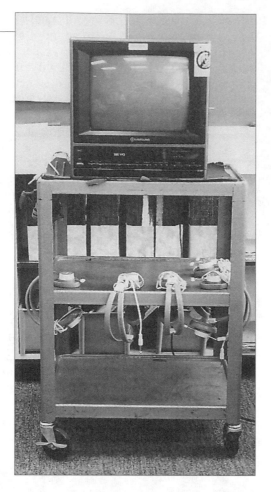

An audiovisual cart supporting the TV/VCR is ideal for both small-group and large-group viewing. It is also easy to move, should you want to connect it to a computer for multimedia work.

When placing the unit in a permanent location, consider that you may occasionally need it for whole-group viewing. Although the screen may be smaller than that of a regular TV, you might position it in such a way that a large group of students could gather around it. To facilitate this option, ensure that the screen is facing into the main area of the classroom. Students can then turn or move their chairs closer for viewing. A large monitor is more appropriate for large-group viewing, of course, but may not always be available.

Speaking/listening equipment

Speaking/listening equipment also requires power outlets, with the exception of hand-held tape recorders operating on rechargeable batteries. In addition to one or more computers with audio input and output capabilities, a large tape recorder and several small ones are a practical combination.

In many schools, students are allowed to move outside the classroom to concentrate on an individual speaking or listening activity and they enjoy being given the responsibility.

A large tape recorder with headphones enables a small group of students to listen to the same selection. Follow-up assignments can vary according to the needs of individual students in the group. Students preparing audio selections for inclusion in multimedia presentations may also need to listen as a small group.

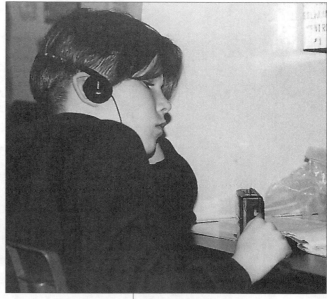

Small hand-held tape recorders are ideal for individual speaking and listening activities.

Other learning areas

The positioning of the technology is interdependent with all of the other components of a successful classroom layout. When you decide to set up workstations for art, science, manipulative mathematics, or design and technology, which involve more than just pencil-and-paper activities, strategic layout is also important. An art workstation should be located near a sink, storage shelves, and supply cupboards. A workstation for concrete, hands-on experiences in science or manipulative mathematics activities also requires storage areas nearby. A design and technology workstation might need ready access to a computer for robotics, programming, or control activities. Some teachers put all of the learning materials for a specific workstation into a large box and assign a student "Materials Manager" to bring the box to and from the workstation. Sometimes students select the floor as the most appropriate place to set up an activity.

As in every work environment, space must be negotiated among all of the users and respected by all. By involving students in the organization of the classroom, the teacher encourages them to participate in making the limited space function as well as possible. It might also be a good idea to invite input from the school custodian!

Floor plans

A floor plan that works well in one technology-integrated classroom may be hopeless in another. Nevertheless, it helps to study sample plans and to borrow or adapt a feature or features that might suit your classroom. Figures 6.1, 6.2, and 6.3 might be helpful.

In arranging the classroom, you will always have to compromise. An ideal arrangement for cooperative learning groups may require that some students will have to turn their chairs around for whole-group lessons. A floor plan that allows all

Figure 6.1

The need for electrical outlets, unless you have floor plugs, dictates that much of the equipment must be placed around the perimeter of the room.

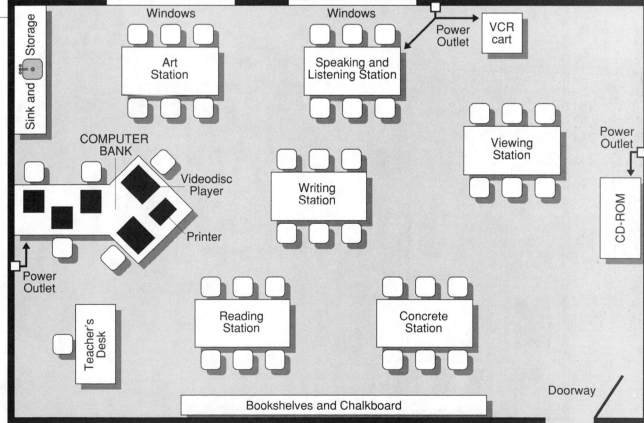

Figure 6.2

In a classroom with only two power outlets, it may be impossible to place enough desks or tables within reach, so students sometimes need to use floor space.

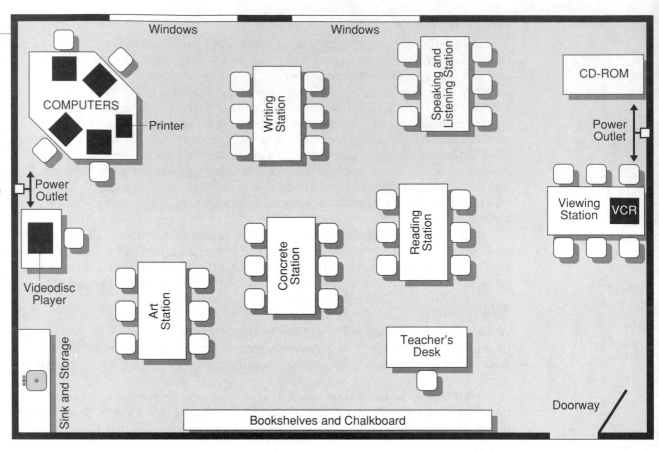

Figure 6.3

By placing tables closer together, it may be possible to leave a large open space for gathering the whole group together.

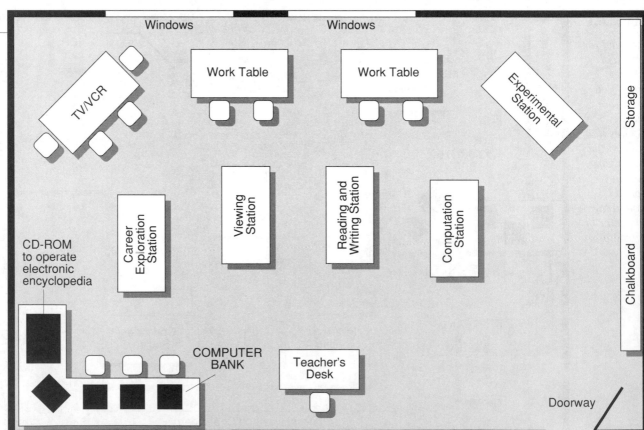

Reprinted with the permission of the Carleton Roman Catholic School Board

students to have an unobstructed view of the chalkboard may necessitate turning around some desks each time you ask the students to work in groups. Some teachers are comfortable with adjusting the spaces in the classroom to meet the needs of the moment. To a certain extent, your flexibility in this regard is governed by the age of your students and the type of furniture in your classroom.

Classroom furniture

Ideally, every technology-integrated classroom would have an adequate number of carts, computer tables, printer stands, audio- and videotape racks, CD holders, and individual carrels for private study. In Chapter 3, "What About Equipment?" we suggested several alternatives in specialized furniture for computers and printers. In reality, however, many classrooms have only student desks and a few assorted tables, but a lack of specialized furniture need not thwart the goal of integrating technology into your program.

Support computers, printers, videodisc players, and TV/VCRs on strong tables, preferably ones that have a shelf underneath so you can keep wires out of the way. You can also place computer paper on this shelf so that it feeds upward into the printer. In a technological classroom, additional tables are required for the larger equipment. You will need an appropriate number of chairs so students can work at these tables.

Tables, with or without shelves, are probably the most adaptable alternative for student seating. Desks with attached chairs are least desirable because they are inflexible and take up a lot of space. You *can* group these desks together to form workstations or cooperative learning areas, but some students find getting in and out of the chairs awkward. Individual desks with detached chairs are easier to group, but if assorted desks are not of uniform height or if the desk tops are sloped, students will not have large, smooth surfaces on which to work. You can try to form seating groups by clustering desks of a standard height.

Some classrooms have cubbyholes or open shelves that provide great storage for students' books, pencil cases, and personal supplies. Cubbyholes can replace individual storage space in desks.

In many classrooms, wheelchair access is a must; a physically or mentally challenged student may need a specific work space that accommodates a personal computer, a communications board, or a walking apparatus. Again, adjustable tables rather than single desks are more likely to suit special-needs students.

Storage facilities

Plastic bins of assorted sizes are very useful in an active, technology-oriented classroom. Use these bins for many purposes, such as to store videocassettes, student notebooks, and batteries that need to be charged. Students can use these to carry books and other materials from one work area to another. Bins can also be used to hold pencils, erasers, scissors, glue sticks, and other items. In general, younger students do not mind sharing these items but older students usually prefer their own materials.

Organizing time

Students need large blocks of time to engage in small-group and individual activities. Subject integration is one way to organize the school day into large blocks of time. The best approach is to present curricular material within holistic contexts rather than segmenting it into separate disciplines. This is particularly true for younger children.

It is frustrating for anyone to get organized for a specific task and then discover there is not enough time to complete it. In technology-oriented classrooms, setup time can be greater than that required to pull out a pencil and paper. For example, it might take five or ten minutes for a student to access the computer network, locate and load the desired program, become reacquainted with the program's procedures and, finally, begin to work. A small group of students might need five or ten minutes to move its chairs and materials to a viewing station, negotiate space for everyone, select a video to watch, plug in headphones, adjust volume controls, and begin the assignment. Setting up a science experiment might take longer still, depending on its complexity. You must take setup procedures into account when planning blocks of time for student work. Setup time is not wasted time. Students learn valuable organizational skills and planning strategies that will one day transfer to a work environment.

There may be times when you do not want to create rigid time boundaries. The open-ended nature of the challenge may be such that you are not sure of exactly what product students will create or how long it will take. By observing carefully, you can identify students who are using their time wisely and those who are having difficulty. Some students require assistance in developing better organizational skills and on-task behavior. Strategies to help these students might include breaking the assignment down into shorter, more specific tasks and providing extra help from a teacher, teacher's aide, or parent helper. In Chapter 9, "Students with Special Needs," additional strategies are provided.

Planning formats

You can select from many different planning formats (see Figures 6.4, 6.5, and 6.6 for examples) to ensure that students have sufficient time for individual pursuits or cooperative learning activities. Students' interest levels, effort, attention, and involvement are enhanced when they have plenty of time to immerse themselves in a theme.

Figure 6.4

This open planning format divides the school day into four quarters.

PLANS FOR: Thursday, February 10		
1. **Opening:** Reflection Anthem Attendance **Language Arts** Novel Study - Chapter 3 1. Introduce vocabulary 2. Together read and discuss the chapter 3. Assignment: Small group - Creation of a story map	R E C E S S	2. **French** Remedial and Planning/Evaluation Time

L U N C H

| 3. **Mathematics**
Introduce 2-digit multiplication
(Use enclosed manipulatives)
Assignments enclosed in math bags
Computer Lab
Objective - To become familiar with the new software program - Around the World | R E C E S S | 4. **Environmental Studies**
Skill - Observing and Researching
1. Students' outside search for insects
2. Observe
3. Carefully capture and label
4. Examine with magnifying glass
5. Use reference materials - CD, videodisc, videotape, text to record information about the insect
Physical Education - See card for warm-up, skills, and game
Basketball Skills - Types of Passes |

Reprinted with the permission of the Carleton Roman Catholic School Board

Figure 6.5

In this planning format, continuity from one day to the next is more apparent than in Figure 6.4.

Week of: October 14–19		
Reminders: Phone Ms. Smith. Speak with the nurse. Meeting with the social worker.		

Duty

Time	Monday	Tuesday
9:00-10:15	**Language Arts/Environmental Studies** • Students take the computer test for Peak Performance • Generate their tracking cards • Organize notebooks	• Together complete an activity from a center • Review classroom procedures and expectations • Divide students into groups • Students start an activity
10:15-10:30	**RECESS**	
10:30-11:20	**Language Arts/Environmental Studies** • Together generate classroom expectations and post	• Students complete activity • Move to next center (Remind students of expectations)
11:20-11:45	**Family Life** • See Family Life Program - pp. 43–45	**Music** • Teacher comes in
11:45-12:45	**LUNCH**	
12:45-1:30	**Mathematics** • Introduce parallel lines • Assignment: Parallel lines in the environment • Software - Lines of All Kinds	1. Correct work from last day 2. Parallel lines in figures 3. Math Text - p. 45 **Physical Education** See attached card for lesson
1:30-2:00	**Physical Education** • See attached card for warm-up, skill, and game	
2:00-2:15	**RECESS**	
2:15-3:30	**French** • Provide assistance to Gr. 4 class Dismissal	**French** • Provide assistance to Gr. 4 class Dismissal

Reprinted with the permission of the Carleton Roman Catholic School Board

Figure 6.6

This planning sheet shows the week at a glance. Each day is divided into three sections.

Week of: March 2–6
Reminders: Contact Mrs. Armstrong, Order replacement disk .
THEME: Conservation   **DATE:** March 6
-Thematic units developed include - Ecosystem Encounter and Facts on the Environment

M O N	**SAMPLE** **Environmental Studies** **1.** Introduce the last knowledge objective - food chains **2.** Students - create food chains **Math** **1.** Introduce 3- by 2-digit multiplication **2.** Environmental questions using multiplication	**Language Arts** Skill - Cause and Effect **1.** Students read environment- related story - The Falcon **2.** Discuss - cause and effect **3.** Assignment - worksheet	**Art** Skill - Use of Primary Colors See sample and directions Family Life Small-Group Work - pages 46–49
T U E	**Environmental Studies** **1.** Students share food chains **2.** They use their knowledge with software Save the Species **Math** **1.** Check work **2.** Video - Multiplication Magic **3.** Students teach one another **4.** Create own problems	**Language Arts** **1.** Correct work **2.** Cartoon strip to show cause/effect **3.** Students explain and display	**French** French teacher takes class **Physical Ed.** - Skill - relay - See card
W E D			
T H U R S			
F R I			

Reprinted with the permission of the Carleton Roman Catholic School Board

Preparing students to use technology

To benefit fully from all that technology offers, students need both direct instruction and freedom to explore. No school or school system can afford the repair bills that result from improper or careless use of equipment. Learning to use a new piece of hardware or software is a hands-on experience requiring time to experiment, or "play," with the technology. This exploration time varies with the complexity of both the hardware and software. When introducing a new computer program of moderate difficulty to 9- to 12-year-old students, for example, we usually recommend 75 minutes in the school's computer lab. This time allotment includes both teacher instruction and student practice. Only after both direct instruction and a period of free exploration should students be expected to use a technology to accomplish a particular task.

A lab setting is the ideal way to introduce computers to beginners and to introduce new software to users at all levels. Instruction in the lab is the easiest way for students to familiarize themselves with something new. Lab instruction works well for large groups. Many teachers find that when students work with a partner in the lab, as opposed to working alone after whole-group instruction, they are more inclined to experiment, to discover, and to learn.

If your school does not have a computer lab, students can gather around a single monitor as you demonstrate a program or a function. They can share practice time on a rotational basis using the classroom computer(s). You will need to set aside several days and plan carefully in order to integrate new hardware and software on a shared basis. Alternatively, if you have only one computer or if the computer lab is unavailable, you can show several key students how to use some new software. These key students can then instruct other students, either individually or in small groups.

Although many students know how to use a TV/VCR and a tape recorder, provide step-by-step instruction for all. Point out the controls and any special features that your students might use. When a group of students shares equipment such as this, designate one student the "Equipment Operator" who will load and unload tapes and adjust controls for brightness and clarity. This method will prevent arguments among group members while safeguarding the equipment from excessive handling.

Specialized equipment such as videodisc players and CD-ROM are not as familiar to students. By rotating students according to a schedule, you can give everyone practice time using this equipment. After a period of free exploration, you could perhaps structure an activity that will guide students in learning the different capabilities of the hardware and software (see Figure 6.7 for an example).

An instruction sheet posted near a piece of equipment serves as an instant reference guide for users, as illustrated in Figure 6.8 on the next page. It also gives students practice in reading and following directions. Reading technical instructions is a valuable skill to develop, one that will help students to pursue lifelong learning in increasingly technological environments.

In every class, one, two, or more students may stand out as having greater technological expertise. (It is important to be aware of gender equity when setting up and using technology.) You could assign these students the roles of helpers, advisers, or troubleshooters. Sometimes more practically minded students are not high academic achievers: assigning them special tasks and responsibilities provides an excellent opportunity to help build their self-esteem and self-confidence. These helpers can be an invaluable human resource in a busy classroom.

Figure 6.7

By doing this activity, students learn how to use one entry path for accessing information in an electronic encyclopedia on CD-ROM. Other activity cards might provide practice using different entry paths and special features of this electronic encyclopedia.

Multimedia Encyclopedia

Activity
#1
Title Finder

Go to the electronic encyclopedia.

Select the TITLE FINDER entry path.

1. Find an article about WRESTLING.

How many pages are in this article?

2. Find an article about HOCKEY, ICE.

What player is shown in the first photograph?

3. Find an article about SOCCER.

What does the diagram on page 3 show?

4. Find an article about BASEBALL.

List the main headings in the table of contents.

5. Find an article about FOOTBALL.

How many books are listed in the bibliography about football?

Figure 6.8

Videodisc players are uncommon in homes and are probably new to most students. For each student to take full advantage of its many features, you can make a poster of selected instructions from the manual and display these in a photo stand or in a folder near the videodisc player as a handy reference.

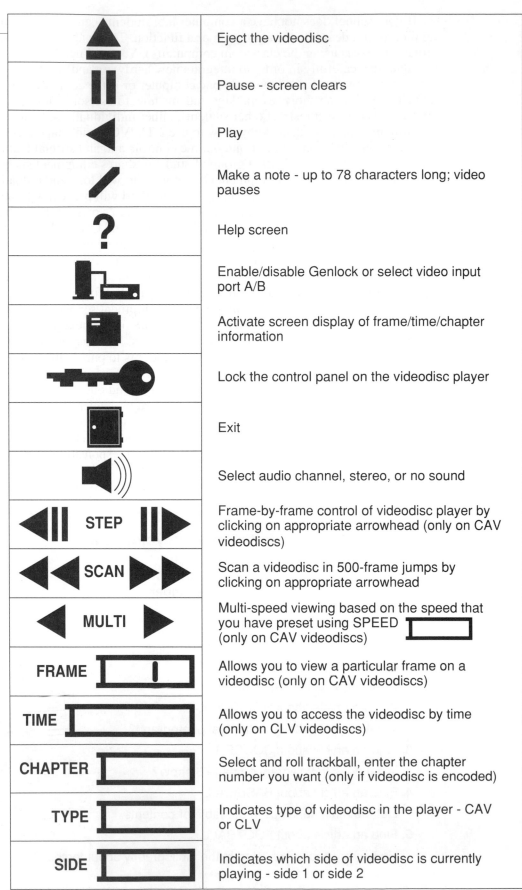

Eject the videodisc

Pause - screen clears

Play

Make a note - up to 78 characters long; video pauses

Help screen

Enable/disable Genlock or select video input port A/B

Activate screen display of frame/time/chapter information

Lock the control panel on the videodisc player

Exit

Select audio channel, stereo, or no sound

STEP — Frame-by-frame control of videodisc player by clicking on appropriate arrowhead (only on CAV videodiscs)

SCAN — Scan a videodisc in 500-frame jumps by clicking on appropriate arrowhead

MULTI — Multi-speed viewing based on the speed that you have preset using SPEED (only on CAV videodiscs)

FRAME — Allows you to view a particular frame on a videodisc (only on CAV videodiscs)

TIME — Allows you to access the videodisc by time (only on CLV videodiscs)

CHAPTER — Select and roll trackball, enter the chapter number you want (only if videodisc is encoded)

TYPE — Indicates type of videodisc in the player - CAV or CLV

SIDE — Indicates which side of videodisc is currently playing - side 1 or side 2

Establishing routines

The introduction of classroom technology makes routines all the more important. These routines, although initiated by the teacher, should be developed in consultation with the students. When students play a role in establishing routines, they enjoy a sense of ownership and responsibility. When one analyzes what actually transpires in a child-centered classroom, it soon becomes obvious that the apparent lack of structure is based on well-established, well-learned, and well-practiced classroom routines.

> ■ If you have ever watched youngsters use Nintendo and other computer games, you know that there are powerful forces at work — concentration, commitment and control. Schools need to harness that power, and technology is the key. With it, students are in control. That [technology] changes the classroom balance of power from a teacher-directed to a student-centred environment. And that promotes learning.[2]

Introduce each type of learning task carefully to the class. The whole group can complete one example of each type of individual assignment as a teacher-directed activity. In this way, the students know exactly what to do and what kinds of outcomes are expected. They know where and within what time frame to accomplish each task. They follow procedures for obtaining necessary materials, using equipment, and putting items away after use. If taking turns or sharing is required, work together to establish procedures for students to follow. Students must know what to do with their completed products and what steps to follow in sharing these products with the rest of the class.

They should also know how to get help when they need it. In many technology-integrated classrooms, students learn to consult with classmates and refer to resource materials before going to the teacher for help (see Figure 6.9). They may follow the rule "Ask three before me." It is also important for students to discover that learning is at times an interactive process in which they learn from talking with one another.

Figure 6.9

By cooperating in the development of a chart of problem-solving strategies, students realize that they are capable of solving many of their own problems. They begin to accept more responsibility for their own learning and your role can evolve into that of facilitator for individualized learning.

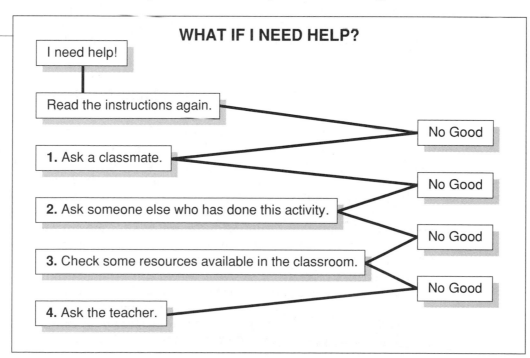

WHAT IF I NEED HELP?

- I need help!
- Read the instructions again. → No Good
- 1. Ask a classmate. → No Good
- 2. Ask someone else who has done this activity. → No Good
- 3. Check some resources available in the classroom. → No Good
- 4. Ask the teacher.

■ In this situation, I become more of the facilitator as opposed to the teacher. They go through a routine of asking other students. If they have difficulty, the other students become the resources for information, for help on the computer or for the CD-ROM. They usually find out what students in the class know that program and ask them before they come to me. (Jim Rogers, teacher)]

Tracking students' work

It is vital to establish a tracking system and to reinforce that every student is accountable for completing certain activities. By placing responsibility for tracking squarely in the hands of students, you encourage them to become more responsible for their own learning. Even very young students can use a simple record sheet to keep track of activities they complete, as illustrated in Blackline Master 6.1. Figure 6.10, on page 92, is an example of a standardized student tracking sheet that can be used by 9- to 12-year-old students to chart their own progress in each unit of study. They must first complete the compulsory activities (indicated by asterisks), which focus on the designated mastery skills of the unit. When they begin an activity, students enter the date and color in half of the small box in the second column; they fill in the other half of the box when they complete the activity. The teacher then initials the sheet and/or offers comments after evaluating the student's work. Following satisfactory completion of the compulsory activities, students can select any other activities of their choice.

After establishing standards for tracking as well as for quality and quantity of work, apply those standards along with appropriate and logical follow-up for work that is not acceptable. These standards vary to suit the range of students within each class, but each student must clearly understand what is expected. As mentioned previously, by doing a variety of different activities as a whole group, you can give students models to follow when they move into independent activities.

The complexity of the tracking system that you design will reflect the level and abilities of your students as well as their experience in managing time. A tracking system must give you specific information: it records the quantity of work being completed by each student on a daily basis and provides a record of the quality of that work.

Preparing parents for technological change

Some parents become anxious when they see a shift away from traditional modes of learning. Understandably, parents want their children to receive the best education possible. The anxiety provoked by change is often rooted in a lack of understanding about the reasons for the change and the precise nature of the change.

Well-articulated goals and strategies, clearly presented to parents at the beginning of the school year, are the best way to allay this anxiety. Parents also need to be consulted on an ongoing basis during the change process and provided with opportunities to learn about the details of technology-integrated programs. In a first-term evening meeting with parents, you can demonstrate your specific classroom strategies and give parents time to absorb and discuss the implications of these strategies. An open house, later in the year when students are comfortable with the equipment, can give them an opportunity to demonstrate their proficiency and their parents a chance to try out the equipment in the classroom for themselves. An open-door policy that invites parents to drop in, watch students at work, interact with them,

BLM 6.1

My name is _____

Week of _____

 **Art**	Paint an animal. Show its home.
 **Listening**	Listen to the story "Is This My Home?"
 **Writing**	Tell where 5 animals live. (A _____ lives in a _____ .)
 **Puzzles and Games**	Play "Animal Bingo" with your friend.
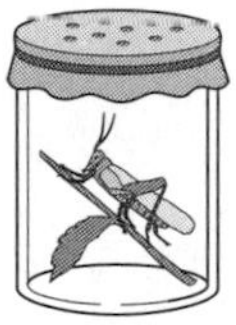 **Science**	Make a home for an insect.
 **Reading**	Read on the computer: "A Home for Harry."
 **Viewing**	Watch the video "Animal Homes."

Figure 6.10

Sample student tracking sheet for 9- to 12-year-old students

TRACKING CARD

Viewing station - ORANGE CARDS

ASSIGNMENT		DATE	COMMENT
*1A			
*1B			
*1C	▨	Nov. 10, 1994	
2A			
2B			
2C	▨	Nov. 9, 1994	Well done, Katie
*3A			
*3B			
*3C			
4A			
4B			
4C			
*5A			
*5B			
*5C			
*6A			
*6B			
*6C			
*7A			
*7B			
*7C			
8			

Concrete Station - YELLOW CARDS

ASSIGNMENT		DATE	COMMENT
*1			
*2A			
*2B			
*2C	▨	Nov. 11, 1994	Correct spelling, please
*3A	▨	Nov. 12, 1994	O.K. DH
3B			
3C			
*4A			
*4B			
*4C			
*5A			
*5B			
*5C			
*6A			
*6B			
*6C			
7			
8			

continued...

Figure 6.10 (cont'd)

TRACKING CARD			
Speaking/Listening Station - GREEN CARDS			
ASSIGNMENT		**DATE**	**COMMENT**
*1A			
*1B			
*1C		Nov. 13, 1994	Good for you. AH
*2A			
*2B		Nov. 13, 1994	
*2C			
*3A			
*3B			
*3C			
*4A			
*4B			
*4C			
*5A			
*5B			
*5C			
*6			
7			

Reprinted with the permission of the Carleton Roman Catholic School Board

and become involved in their learning will do much to alleviate parental concerns. Ongoing communication is the key.

Parents need to receive the distinct message that we are preparing students for a different world, one in which they must continue to learn throughout their lives in order to adapt to technology-oriented working and living environments.

Typical parent questions

From our experience in conducting a large number of meetings and discussions with parents and other community members, we can predict many of the questions you may be asked. It is helpful to think about some of these issues in advance, so here are some commonly asked questions, along with some helpful hints for composing answers.

Q. With what technology will my child work?

A. Be well informed as to the manufacturers, models, and capabilities of the technology because today's parent community is very knowledgeable; however, do not be afraid to admit that your knowledge has limits and that you rely on experts in the field to provide you with information.

Q. What computer system are you using?

A. Answer in a direct way without voicing support for one brand of computer over another, because the moment you praise the superiority of one particular brand, someone will disagree with you. You do not want your discussion to turn into a technical argument about computer platforms. It is more important to stress the general benefits that computers bring to education and the fact that the opportunity for students to work with any computer will make the transition to other makes and models easier.

Q. What research has been done on incorporating technology into the classroom?

A. Be able to support what you are doing with current education research. This proves that you have done your homework and instills confidence in you as an educator. Some parents might appreciate receiving a current article or reading list.

Q. What skills are being taught?

A. With the emphasis today on mastery learning, benchmarks, and learning outcomes, parents will want to know what subject-specific skills are being taught, so be ready with a list. This is also an ideal opportunity to emphasize the value of cooperative learning skills, thinking skills, and, of course, technology-related skills.

Q. How much does it cost?

A. As parents and taxpayers they have the right to know; however, the process is not always as simple as citing an amount. Be sure to include the grant process involved and any special business/education partnerships. Members of your audience may be able to assist you in financing your innovation or may know someone else who can help.

Q. What does the teacher do?

A. Some people see the teacher eventually being replaced by technology. Highlight the changing role of the teacher in the technological classroom. The job is not becoming simpler, but more complex.

Q. How do you individualize my child's program?

A. If you have referred to individualizing the student's program, be prepared to explain in detail how this occurs.

Q. My child has special needs. How are they addressed in this classroom?

A. Parents of special-needs students are frequently concerned that their children are receiving the required support. You might want to outline some general ways that technology can help students with special needs. The individual needs, however, are usually so specific that you may wish to speak to these parents in detail in a less public forum.

Q. What if my child needs help using the technology?

A. Be ready to explain the classroom routines that are in place to address the immediate concerns that students may have. Again, highlight the variety of roles of the teacher in a technology-oriented classroom and the opportunities for one-to-one interaction.

Q. Are the arts being neglected in a technology-enhanced program?

A. Be prepared to show evidence of the balance among mathematics, science and technology, language arts, and the fine arts in your daily program. Music, art, and drama are not at risk because of the introduction of technology into the classroom; in fact, the teaching of each can be enhanced through the use of technology.

Q. Is my child at a disadvantage in not having a computer at home?

A. Be very sensitive to the fact that not all parents have the financial resources to purchase a home computer. Stress instead the important point that the student has access to computer technology at school. If your school has noon-hour or after-school programs in which students can access computers, this is the time to draw parents' attention to these opportunities.

Q. What kind of computer should I buy?

A. This question is a difficult one. Ideally, the student's home computer would be compatible with the school's system so that work can be transferred. However, many different family members may want to use the computer for a variety of purposes, so each situation is unique. The family should consider all of the proposed uses for the computer and buy something that meets its needs.

Q. What software should I buy?

A. For parents, selecting a piece of software can mean considering a number of factors such as price, ease of access, flashy graphics, packaging, or even what a neighbor has chosen. It is not necessary to talk in specifics here unless there are some pieces of software that you really want a student to use at home to complete or complement in-school assignments. You may have seen a particular program that you can recommend or you may want to prepare a list of some general guidelines for the selection of software, such as the following:

- Is it age-appropriate?
- Does it begin at a level that is realistic for your child's present grade level?
- Does it have enough scope to last your child through several more grade levels?
- Does it provide a wide variety of activities?
- Is it easy for the child to use?
- Does it have visual appeal (and auditory, if your equipment allows for it)?
- Are skills introduced in a logical and sequential manner?
- Are feedback and/or rewards given to the child for success along the way?
- Is the child required to think and use problem-solving skills?
- Can you customize the program to meet specific needs?

Suggest that parents take part in using computer programs with their children, just as they would when reading a book.

■ "I think it's important that parents do not use the computer as an alternative to TV," said Ronald Ragdale, a professor in the department of measurement, evaluation and computer application at the Ontario Institute for Studies in Education in Toronto. "If parents approach this with the idea that I'm going to get something to teach my children so that I don't have to teach my children, they will be disappointed."[3]

CHAPTER 7

The Well-Mannered, Safe, Technological Classroom

When students make choices and decisions about their learning, they are motivated to continue the process. They are accountable and responsible for their own learning and make decisions that reflect upon themselves directly.... Establishing rules and routines before specific assignments are initiated provides the structure necessary for this type of learning.[1]

Teachers often wonder how a classroom environment can be established that promotes respect and a sense of shared responsibility for the care of the technology. Also, with schools being increasingly used as community centers and to provide recreational and meeting facilities, security of equipment becomes even more important. Student safety is also of paramount concern in the technological classroom, particularly that of younger students. Consider not only electrical safety and safe movement around a crowded classroom, but also physical safety — proper positioning and posture for students who may spend long periods of time sitting at computers.

Establishing equipment care and protection routines

Whenever students are required to share equipment, materials, and space, routines are necessary. Classes will vary in the extent to which care and respect for the equipment need to be taught. Even with the most responsible students, however, begin the year with a discussion of how equipment should be treated. To encourage students to feel responsible for "their" equipment, they should be the ones to develop the guidelines for its care and use. Have small groups of students brainstorm lists of do's and don'ts for the various pieces of equipment in the classroom. A "Take Care of Our Computers" chart, for example, might include some of the ideas illustrated in Blackline Master 7.1. Discuss, modify, add to, agree on, and post these rules in the classroom. Discussing and posting these guidelines does not mean that they will always be followed, however. You will undoubtedly need to review, reinforce, and apply logical consequences for students who habitually show disrespect for school property. Verbal pressure from teachers and peers is often enough to deter a student who has difficulty following established routines. The final consequence for the student who continually abuses equipment is loss of the privilege of using it for a given length of time.

BLM 7.1

Do not bring food or drink near the computers.

Tap the keys — do not bang them.

Do not just turn off the computer — exit from programs by closing files in sequence.

Hands off the keyboard except when you are working on it.

Do not mix water, paint, and computers.

Move carefully around the computer tables.

Be patient — tap the ENTER key only once, then wait.

Never use anyone else's login.

Cleanliness

Care of equipment also includes cleanliness. Wires that drag on the ground are traps for dust and dirt. You can bundle them up and attach them to table legs using fasteners, twist-ties, or tape, although tape does not usually last very long. The school custodian will appreciate attention to this seemingly small detail.

Dust is the enemy of all electronic equipment and classrooms are notoriously dusty places, due to the sheer number of feet that move in, out, and around them daily. Chalk dust adds to the problem, so do not place computers close to chalkboards. Dust collects in computer keyboards and the switches and buttons of other equipment. Not only does this make them unpleasant to use, but it also leads to mechanical problems over a period of time. Some schools have substituted whiteboards to reduce the amount of classroom dust.

Keep small equipment in plastic bags when not in use. An ambitious parent group could undertake the task of sewing some simple computer covers for you if the school cannot afford to buy them. An old bed sheet draped over the computers at night will be good enough to help protect them from the dust and dirt that is stirred up when the classroom is swept. A student should be given the job of covering and uncovering them, and students can also take responsibility for dusting the computers, especially the screens, on a weekly basis or as required. The more students are involved in the care of the equipment, the more respect they will have for it.

Storage and security of equipment

Organized and efficient techniques for the storage of equipment help students to take care of it, make it more accessible, and contribute to security measures. You cannot afford to take any risks regarding security. Chances are that if something is lost or stolen, it may not be replaced for a long time. Without equipment, the program suffers. If you decide to move on to another class or school, you will surely be asked for an accounting of all of the equipment that has been provided.

Large equipment

Large equipment such as VCRs, computers, and videodisc players should be secured to tables or counters in a permanent way. Most schools use cables and locks for this purpose. If the piece of equipment has nothing for the cable to go through, a U-bolt may have to be attached for this purpose, as shown in the photo on page 33 in Chapter 3. A professional thief would be able to remove these locks and cables, but they will serve to discourage vandals or others who may be in the school after hours for assorted reasons.

All equipment should be engraved with the school name and an identification number or mark placed inside the machine or outside in an inconspicuous spot, since serial numbers can be easily eradicated. A description of this identifying mark will serve as proof that the machine belongs to you should the police be able to reclaim it after a theft. An updated list of all serial numbers should be maintained, however.

Equipment that is highly visible is bound to be a temptation to thieves. Always close the curtains and blinds at the end of the day. If the school is often used for evening activities, lock classrooms that will not be used. During the long summer holidays when various strangers are in and out of schools, it is wise to take all of the expensive equipment out of the classroom and lock it away in a secure storage room. In some schools, all large equipment is kept on trolleys or movable tables and putting it away is a daily event. Students could take turns being responsible for storing and retrieving the equipment as part of the daily classroom routine.

Small equipment

Small items, such as hand-held tape recorders, batteries, calculators, language masters, computer disks, CDs, audio- and videotapes, headphones, and videodiscs, require careful storage. When several students are in the process of setting up for an activity, they need to be able to get the required materials without interfering with one another, without arguments, and without a great deal of noise and fuss. They also need to be able to return materials easily and neatly, leaving them ready for use by someone else.

Also, it is the small equipment that most frequently disappears, such as hand-held calculators and CDs. It is wise to set up some type of storage system that allows you to ensure at a glance that the correct number of items is present. For example, hand-held tape recorders can be stored in individual plastic bags. Each bag might also contain a set of headphones and an adapter for plugging the unit into the wall outlet. This way, everything required is in one place and can be set up quickly by a student for the task at hand. The bags can then be stored in a pocket chart or hung on hooks on a pegboard, making it easy to ensure that they are all there. Small calculators can also be stored in this manner.

Plastic cases protect audiotapes and keep them clean, but the cases are often quite brittle and will not stand up to rough treatment. If they are loose in a bin, students have to root through them to find the one they want, breaking cases and ultimately damaging the tapes themselves. An alternative is to purchase an inexpensive audiocassette holder that allows the tapes to be held in grooves and also has the advantage of exposing the labels for readability. A cheaper but short-term solution is to mount adhesive-backed book pockets on a sheet of cardboard or a bulletin board and label each with the name of the tape that it contains.

Bags holding small tape recorders or calculators can be put into a pocket chart, securely attached to a wall so that the weight is safely supported. When stored this way, it is easy to ensure that the proper number of pieces of small equipment is on hand.

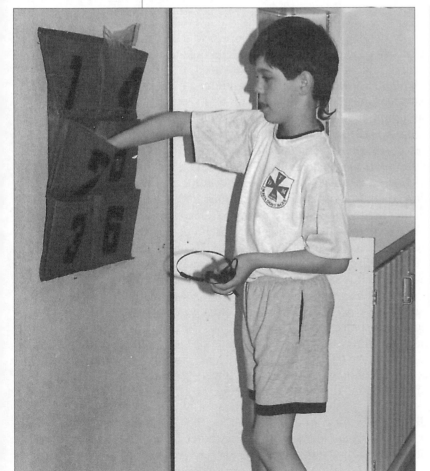

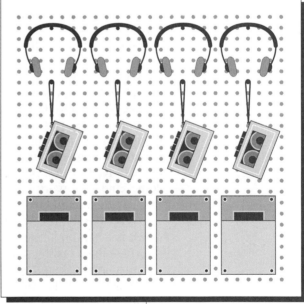

A pegboard can be mounted with hooks and templates that show the location of each piece of small equipment.

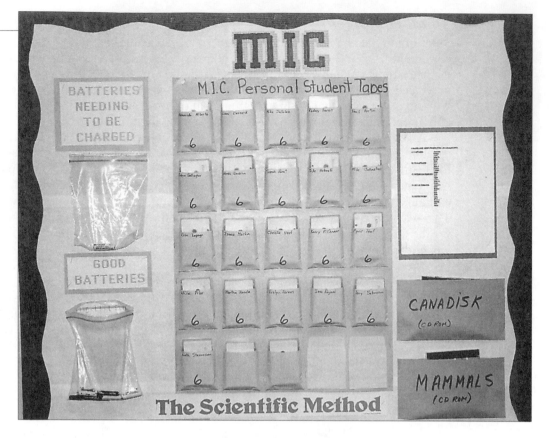

Individual student tapes or listening tapes may be conveniently stored in book pockets, but paper pockets are not likely to last through the whole school year.

Videotapes tend to have more durable cases than audiotapes, so they can be stored in a box or bin. Be sure to label each case on the outside so that students do not have to waste time opening and closing cases to find the video they need. A variety of inexpensive video racks are available, or maybe a parent could donate one.

Headphones can be a nuisance if the cords are always tangled. Younger students often delight in pulling and stretching them to make them pop free. Teach students to wind the cords around the headphone before putting them away in a box or bin, or hang each set of headphones from a wall hook and let the cords hang free. Our favorite storage idea for headphones is to suspend a large hoop from the ceiling.

CD-ROMs, computer disks, and videodiscs usually come in folders or cases of some kind. It is worth investing some time in training your students to handle these items with care and to replace them in their containers after use. Once again, an inexpensive rack is often the best storage solution, and clear labeling is important.

It is desirable to minimize the amount of direct handling of CDs and videodiscs. If the students are using only one videodisc during a unit of study, it may be best to leave that disc inside the player at all times. It is safe and ready to use, and it stays clean.

A plastic carrier of some sort may be required to insert a CD-ROM into the computer. If so, your school would be wise to invest in some extra carriers so that each CD can remain protected and dust-free in a carrier instead of students having to switch different CDs back and forth from case to carrier as they need them. In some schools, this is not a problem because the CD-ROM capabilities are managed through towers located centrally, usually in the library. A librarian or library technician is responsible for loading and unloading and the CD is accessed in the classroom by way of a network.

If there are assorted small items left lying around the room at the end of the day, such as CDs or a spell master, try to develop the habit of tucking them into a file cabinet or desk drawer so that they are not visible to anyone passing by the door to the classroom. It takes only a moment and it is time well spent.

A hoop hung from the ceiling at a comfortable height for students makes headphones easy to store and they remain tangle-free.

Batteries

If you have equipment that requires batteries (e.g., language/spell master, external speakers for a CD-ROM), you will need to introduce a system not only for storing those batteries, but for keeping them sorted as to whether they are charged or not charged. One system is to label two small plastic bins or baggies as "Charged" and "Needs Charging." When a student removes dead batteries from a piece of equipment, he or she can simply drop them into the "Needs Charging" bin and insert new ones from the "Charged" bin.

You need enough extra batteries that you do not run out of charged ones on any given day. A student can be given the task of placing the batteries needing charging into the battery charger at the end of the day and taking them out the following morning for deposit into the "Charged" bin. Once this routine is established, it will continue smoothly and lack of charged batteries will not become a source of frustration. Do keep in mind that rechargeable batteries should never be charged until they have *completely* run down.

Safety guidelines

Since you are responsible for the safety of each student who enters your classroom, do not hesitate to approach an appropriate person in your school if you are unsure about the safety of any of the equipment. This person might be a school administrator, the health and safety officer, or perhaps the custodian. The following are basic electrical safety guidelines, some of which are illustrated in Blackline Master 7.2:

- Electrical circuits should not be overloaded by the use of more than one power bar.
- One power bar should not be connected to another.
- Extension cords should not run across doorways or any other areas where people walk.
- Extension cords should not run around sinks or water fountains.
- Cords running around the perimeter of walls should be hooked or taped securely in place.
- Cords should not dangle down where people's feet are likely to tangle in them.
- Electrical cords should not run under carpets.
- Cords should be checked regularly for signs of wear or fraying.

Time is well spent reviewing electrical safety rules with students. The younger the students, the more time will be required. You may want to cooperatively develop some electrical safety rules for the classroom, which might include:

- Never poke around inside any electrical machine.
- Keep liquids away from electrical equipment.
- Do not touch a plug, a switch, or any electrical machine with wet hands.
- Never touch an electrical plug or cord that is broken or frayed.
- Never place anything into an electrical outlet except a plug.
- When plugging in or unplugging a piece of equipment from an outlet, hold the plug carefully. Do not pull it out by the cord.

Once they are alerted to be aware of electrical safety, students need only periodic reminders. They will be quick to tell you if they notice any potentially dangerous situations or behaviors.

Student behavior is particularly important in a classroom in which technology limits the amount of space. While moving around the room, students have to navigate through assorted groupings of tables and chairs. Take advantage of any available space outside of the classroom to expand your work area.

The safety of students and equipment alike can be threatened by rough play or pushing. It is easy for a student to trip, fall, or get bumped in a classroom that is crowded. An active learning environment requires movement, but the confined space within which this movement must take place necessitates certain guidelines. Through open discussions and problem-solving interaction with students, these guidelines can be established, maintained, and changed as required. Courtesy and politeness are essential skills in the technological classroom. Respect for others is a social goal that you can develop and encourage through classroom lessons, conflict-resolution strategies, and cooperative learning activities.

Ergonomics

In the days of the typewriter, typing classes included instruction about correct posture and the appropriate height for equipment. As evidence mounts about health problems associated with computer use, teachers and students need to be reminded that good

One power bar should not be connected to another.

Cords should not dangle down where people's feet are likely to tangle in them.

Extension cords should not run across doorways or any other areas where people walk.

Cords should be checked regularly for signs of wear.

keyboarding posture and positioning is necessary to avoid the possibility of serious injury. Teach and model correct posture (see Blackline Master 7.3), and follow these guidelines in placing keyboards and monitors:

- When keyboarding, students' arms should be at about a right angle, level, with flat wrists;
- Wrists should not rest on the keyboard or table;
- Position screens at eye level and an arm's length away.

With so many students of varying sizes in one classroom, how can correct positioning be achieved for all? One solution is to have adjustable chairs and/or tables, but these are expensive. It might be more feasible to have cushions of varying thicknesses available. Making them would be a worthwhile project for a parent group or senior life skills/home economics class.[2]

Troubleshooting tips

When first working with computers, we found that there were many little things that could go wrong. These hints for new "techies" might make your life easier and help to avoid some frustration. It is a good idea to share these types of simple tips with your students so that they can do some troubleshooting before calling you for help. Blackline Master 7.4 on page 106 will help to reinforce some of these.

- If a machine does not work at all, first ascertain that every piece of equipment and any required power bars are turned on. Next, check the cables to see if they are all connected. Wiggle the wires to see if you are experiencing a poor connection.
- If you change cabling or electrical connections, turn the computer(s) off to make the change. Try to isolate a problem by changing only one thing at a time, and check the equipment after each change.
- If a disk does not work, check that the disk you are using is for the type of computer you are using.
- If a program does not load or run correctly, turn everything off. Then turn everything on again and start all over.
- If you are not able to access all of the features of a program, check to see that you have the correct version for the amount of memory available.
- Before you print, always save your material on a disk or the hard drive of the computer.
- To protect your work, make a backup copy of all important data.
- To prevent someone else from writing on your disks, use write-protect tabs. Check to make sure the tabs are securely fastened so they do not jam or come off in the disk drive.
- To protect your disks and computers, do not put magnets or magnetized objects near them. The magnetization could damage the contents.
- To ensure that disks retain their usefulness, do not leave them in direct sunlight or very hot or cold places for long periods of time.

BLM 7.3

If a program does not load or run correctly, turn everything off and start all over again.

Before you print, always save your material on a disk or the hard drive of the computer.

To protect your disks and computers, do not put magnets or magnetized objects near them.

To protect your work, make a backup copy of all important data.

To ensure that disks retain their usefulness, do not leave them in direct sunlight or very hot or cold places for long periods of time.

CHAPTER 8

Evaluating Student Progress

Not everything that counts can be counted and not everything that can be counted counts.[1]

Why do we evaluate? A common reason is to provide parents, guardians, and other educators with important and useful information. This becomes more critical when you are working with a technology-enhanced curriculum that may appear to be very different from the curriculum experienced by parents. Another important reason to evaluate is to motivate students to improve by providing constructive feedback. This recognizes the student as an active participant in the teaching/learning process. Evaluation can also identify strengths and weaknesses that will help you to modify your teaching and/or curriculum to better meet the needs of each student, asking yourself such questions as: Is there a more effective way to develop this skill? What could I do differently next time?

Figure 8.1

Evaluation is a cyclical process in which the interpretation of observations provides the basis for program planning and implementation.

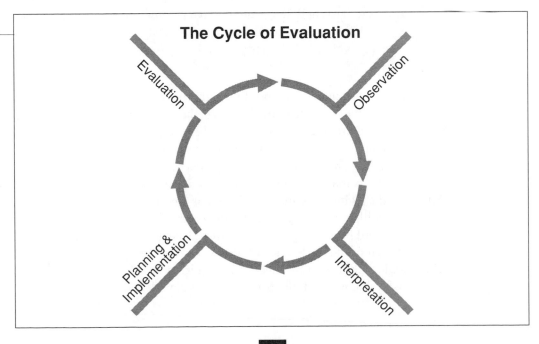

The Cycle of Evaluation

Evaluation

Observation

Interpretation

Planning & Implementation

The importance of formal testing as an evaluation strategy varies greatly from school to school and is influenced by factors such as grade level, type of subject matter, and parent-reporting format. Many teachers are frustrated in their attempts to fully utilize information technologies because they are caught in an evaluation system focusing only on traditional skills.

> ■ Until the day comes when our tests finally measure the skills needed for the 21st century, teachers can be expected to teach the traditional skills of the 19th and mid-20th centuries. That is how their performance is judged. That is what matters. Who can blame them for behaving like intelligent organisms, putting their efforts where they pay off?[3]

This chapter examines some other strategies for evaluation in an active, student-centered, technology-enhanced classroom where students are encouraged to take responsibility for their own learning. We also suggest some ways that technology can assist teachers in assessing and evaluating student progress.

What to evaluate in the technological classroom

You need to know what you are looking for in order to find it. Unit planning forms the basis for evaluation. When you plan a unit of study, you designate desired learning outcomes related to specific knowledge, instructional skills, thinking skills, technological skills, and attitudes. As students work through the different components of a curriculum unit, the development of knowledge, skills, and attitudes is improved through regular feedback. Remember to tell students what knowledge, skills, and attitudes are expected as outcomes of a unit. Many times, we assume that students already know this information or perhaps do not need to know. Even very young children should understand what is expected of them and why it is important.

> ■ If report cards and marks are to have meaning for the future, they must measure achievement of results on complex tasks and in actual performance, not just the acquisition of knowledge and theory.[2]

Evaluation includes both product and process. As you examine the students' products, you will be able to evaluate whether they have a significant grasp of the knowledge and are developing some of the selected skills. By observing the process, you will be able to determine the development of attitudes and a different array of skills, including creative thinking and problem solving.

Some skills that affect both product and process might relate to using technology. Although the technology may be viewed as simply the tool to do the job, skills are associated with technology, such as keyboarding and the ability to use a variety of software (word processing, graphics, spreadsheets). Many report cards now require an evaluation of the student's attitude toward technology and/or the specific technological skills that the student is acquiring. In addition, these skills are important and transferable when students move into the work force.

Types of evaluation

In an active, student-centered, technology-enhanced learning environment, evaluation can take many forms. To obtain a truly authentic assessment, most teachers rely on a variety of data-gathering methods such as teacher observation, self- and peer evaluation, teacher-student conferencing, evaluation of daily work, and tests. Technology can help you to evaluate, record, and organize portfolios that allow you to communicate better with parents.

Teacher observation

Formal observation can be used to obtain data for both formative and summative evaluation. During whole-group sessions, you may want to evaluate how well a student follows directions or contributes to class discussions. Cooperative learning activities provide an opportunity for you to move into the role of observer as the groups pursue carefully planned and structured tasks. While students are working at individual pursuits, you may want to observe different skills, such as how well a student follows written instructions, works independently, or exhibits on-task behavior.

It is not practical to try to look at all behaviors at the same time; target one or two for observation. A formal observation sheet such as the one shown in Blackline Master 8.1 on the next page is useful for recording observations, but consider also how technology can be used to enhance these observations. Video- and audiotaping are excellent ways of gathering observational data. Busy teachers, however, can rarely divorce themselves from student needs in order to gather such data. Assigning this task to a student teacher, teacher helper, or teacher assistant provides an opportunity for them to improve their observational skills, while at the same time providing you with important data for reporting and feedback to parents.

We suggest that you let the students know what is being observed so that they will attempt to practice and thus better learn these behaviors. The special abilities, interests, and needs of each student are most clearly evident through careful observation. Over a period of time, you will gather a profile of social/behavioral skills for each student. Some techniques for observing children working either with or without technology include the following:

- Observe for something specific. Have a focus (e.g., ease with which the student is able to locate a specific piece of software, load it, and start working).
- Choose a couple of students and observe them throughout an entire day: How often do they choose to use technology for particular tasks? How familiar are they with operating a given piece of equipment?
- Observe as a spectator without interacting.
- Observe as a participant while working with the student.
- Develop a realistic plan that will allow you to gradually observe all students over a period of time.
- Make notes and keep records of what has been observed — date all records.
- Use technology to help you in observing (e.g., tape individual student reading samples, videotape group work).
- Use technology to help you in recording student marks (e.g., use a word processing program, a spreadsheet, and/or grade-management software for efficiency in ongoing record-keeping).

BLM 8.1

COLLABORATIVE SKILLS CHECKLIST

Student's Name	contributes and shares materials and equipment	takes turns	uses quiet voice, calm manner	encourages others to contribute	listens carefully to others' ideas	criticizes "positively"	other skills	describes feelings	suggests use of technological resources	gives direction to group's work	explains concepts and instructions	asks for information	relieves tension by joking	accepts criticism	

Reprinted with the permission of the Carleton Roman Catholic School Board

Figure 8.2

The teacher need only move the bar code reader across a student's bar code and the appropriate skill and qualifier when a relevant observation is made. At the end of the day, the bar-code reader is plugged into the computer and the stored data is downloaded into student files.

Computer software combined with bar-code technology can be used to create student profiles from teacher observations. The teacher has an observation sheet (see Figure 8.2) that lists the students' names, plus bar-coded observations such as "writes in complete sentences" and qualifiers such as "developing with difficulty" or "developing as expected." There may also be bar-coded "blanks" where the teacher can type in other observations not included in the list.

Observation, when used as a formative assessment tool, involves more than the word implies, because observation is only the first step in the process. Observation is followed by evaluation and then a decision as to appropriate action:

- You notice that Jenny is skipping from screen to screen through a computer program instead of following the instructions given.
- Evaluate this behavior: maybe she is bored, preoccupied with personal problems, does not understand the instructions, or the content is too difficult.
- Once the reason is discovered, you can decide on appropriate action.

Student	Observations	Qualifiers
Terry Gervais	Writes in complete sentences.	Highly developed.
Mark Brown	Uses appropriate end punctuation.	Developing as expected.
Maria Lopez	Uses capital letters to begin sentences, for proper nouns, and for headings.	Developing with difficulty.
Leslie Watson	Uses a variety of resources (print and non-print) to obtain information.	Not yet developed.
Keiko Hotta	Proofreads and edits own work.	
Caroline Zenner		

Student self-evaluation

A self-evaluation component is also important. In order for this strategy to be effective, invest some time in developing the techniques and skills of self-evaluation with your students. The frequency with which you use self-evaluation will depend on your comfort level, the time available, the particular students, and the type of learning goals. Self-evaluation can help students to focus on their own strengths and weaknesses. Even very young children can be given the opportunity to evaluate their own progress.

Various types of self-evaluation sheets are helpful in both individual and group work, such as those shown in Blackline Masters 8.2 through 8.5. In the "Other" section in Blackline Master 8.2, the teacher could add specific resources that had been suggested to the students and/or particular social skills that the group was assigned to practice while completing an activity.

A group-evaluation sheet, such as the one shown in Blackline Master 8.5 on page 116, provides the opportunity for the students to cooperatively reflect on their work and decide how to improve their teamwork. For younger students, only items 1 through 5 of the evaluation sheet could be used and pictures provided for their responses, such as the faces in Blackline Master 8.4 on page 115.

An electronic portfolio of student-selected samples of writing, saved on computer disk, provides an excellent summary of writing progress. Students can also write passages on the computer, critique their own work with or without teacher input, and add this to their individual profiles. The same can be done with oral work if you have a computer with recording and playback capabilities.

Peer evaluation

Peer evaluation is a technique that can be extremely powerful but must be used with care. For example, you should discuss honesty, fairness, and objectivity with students before allowing them to evaluate one another. Opportunities arise daily for both formal and informal peer evaluation when students present their completed products to others. Use a formal framework for constructive comments (Blackline Master 8.6 on page 117 is an example of this) and teach effective evaluation methods to students if you expect them to evaluate one another. Keep peer evaluations confidential and stress respect for others' rights when using this technique.

Teacher-student conferencing

When students are working individually, you can use teacher-student conferencing as an evaluation technique. Conferencing may or may not involve a student's written work. Conferencing is not necessarily happening every time the teacher marks completed work in the student's presence; true conferencing is much more. In talking with the student about an assignment, whether finished or unfinished, you can discover the degree of understanding of a concept, assist in the development of a skill, or challenge a student to reach farther. It is in this setting that you grow in understanding and appreciation of the uniqueness of each individual.

Journal writing can be a form of conferencing — it enables you to evaluate student attitudes and degree of understanding of concepts. Some form of response from the teacher is vital to encourage and maintain student journal writing. An electronic journal, such as the one illustrated in Figure 8.3, on page 118, might make this process easier.

Self-Checking My Work

Name: _____ Date: _____

Circle the number that best describes your work on the activity you have just completed. Try to be fair and honest.

5 Excellent
4 Very Good
3 Good
2 Satisfactory
1 Poor

1. Effort
- I tried as hard as I could.   1   2   3   4   5
- I looked for help when I had difficulty.   1   2   3   4   5
- I helped someone else in the group.   1   2   3   4   5

2. Use of Resources
- I used books.   1   2   3   4   5
- I contacted people.   1   2   3   4   5
- I used technology.   1   2   3   4   5

3. Amount of Work
- I contributed to the group.   1   2   3   4   5
- I listened to others.   1   2   3   4   5
- I took responsibility for a task. 1   2   3   4   5

4. Use of Time
- I did not waste my time.   1   2   3   4   5
- I did not waste anyone else's time. 1   2   3   4   5
- I finished in the time allowed.   1   2   3   4   5

5. Other
- _____   1   2   3   4   5
- _____   1   2   3   4   5

Choose one item from the ones listed above in which you think you could improve. What could you do differently next time?

_____
_____
_____
_____
_____

My Work Habits

Name: _____ Date: _____

Rate your own work habits for this month.
Read each sentence and circle the number that best describes your work habits.

3 Always
2 Sometimes
1 Seldom

1. I try to do my best.	3 2 1
2. I listen carefully in class.	3 2 1
3. I follow directions well.	3 2 1
4. I use my time well.	3 2 1
5. I keep up to date on my homework assignments.	3 2 1
6. My work is neat and organized.	3 2 1
7. I study for tests a few days in advance.	3 2 1
8. I use the best tools for the job.	3 2 1
9. I contribute to class discussions.	3 2 1
10. I keep my mind on my work.	3 2 1

I Can Do It

Name: _____ Date: _____

1. I can read by myself.

2. I can write stories by myself.

3. I do my best work.

4. I listen to the teacher.

5. I listen to my friends.

6. I use my time well.

7. I like to use the computer.

8. I learn many new things.

Evaluation Sheet for Small-Group Activities

Team: _____ Date: _____

Agree on your answers as a group. Circle your choice.

1. Did we share?   YES   SOMETIMES   NO

2. Did we take turns?   YES   SOMETIMES   NO

3. Did everyone contribute?   YES   NO

4. Did we listen to each other?   YES   SOMETIMES   NO

5. Did we help each other?   YES   SOMETIMES   NO

Finish each sentence.

6. We agreed on _____

7. We disagreed on _____

8. We each had a task. The tasks were:

STUDENT NAME	TASK

9. We could improve by _____

_____

_____

_____

BLM 8.6

Observing Others' Work

Name: _____ Date: _____

Student who is being evaluated: _____

Circle the number that best describes the student's work on the activity just completed. Try to be fair and honest.

5 Excellent
4 Very Good
3 Good
2 Satisfactory
1 Poor

1. Effort
- Concentrated on the task.   1 2 3 4 5
- Looked for help when having difficulty.   1 2 3 4 5
- Helped someone else in the group.   1 2 3 4 5

2. Use of Resources
- Used books.   1 2 3 4 5
- Contacted people.   1 2 3 4 5
- Used technology.   1 2 3 4 5

3. Amount of Work
- Contributed to the group.   1 2 3 4 5
- Listened to others.   1 2 3 4 5
- Took responsibility for a task.   1 2 3 4 5

4. Use of Time
- Did not waste my time.   1 2 3 4 5
- Did not waste others' time.   1 2 3 4 5
- Finished in the time allowed.   1 2 3 4 5

5. Other
- _____   1 2 3 4 5
- _____   1 2 3 4 5

Choose one item from the ones listed above in which you think that this student could improve. Suggest what the student might do differently next time.

_____

_____

_____

_____

_____

Figure 8.3

This journal functions like a word processor. Students must analyze and clarify their ideas about the mathematics they are learning in order to communicate them to the teacher.

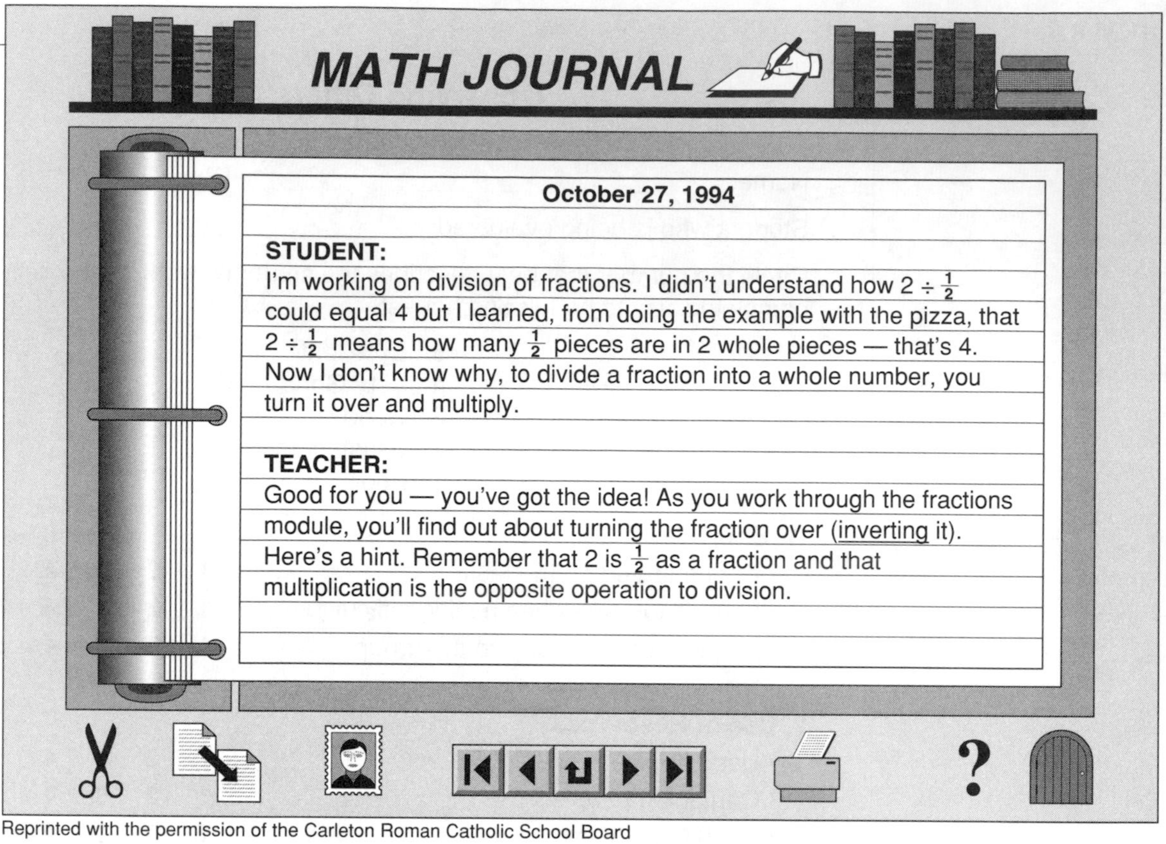
MATH JOURNAL
October 27, 1994
STUDENT:
I'm working on division of fractions. I didn't understand how $2 \div \frac{1}{2}$ could equal 4 but I learned, from doing the example with the pizza, that $2 \div \frac{1}{2}$ means how many $\frac{1}{2}$ pieces are in 2 whole pieces — that's 4. Now I don't know why, to divide a fraction into a whole number, you turn it over and multiply.
TEACHER:
Good for you — you've got the idea! As you work through the fractions module, you'll find out about turning the fraction over (inverting it). Here's a hint. Remember that 2 is $\frac{1}{2}$ as a fraction and that multiplication is the opposite operation to division.
?

Reprinted with the permission of the Carleton Roman Catholic School Board

Daily work

Daily work can be evaluated by the teacher, by peers, or by the student. It is an impossible task for a teacher to mark every piece of work completed by every student every day. In addition, the marking in an individualized program is even more time-consuming than in a more traditional program, because each student is completing a different task. However, students can mark their own and each other's work.

Evaluation shared between teacher and students is consistent with an attitude of shared responsibility. You may want to mark particular assignments that address mastery skills and to review those that have been student-corrected. The ideal time to mark a student's work is immediately on completion, while the work is still fresh in the student's mind and correction and re-teaching are meaningful. You could perhaps focus on two particular workstations for marking each day.

■ I have the students put their names on a sign-up sheet as soon as they have an assignment that needs to be marked by me, then I call them to come over when I'm available. This way, students are not wasting time standing in line waiting for me when they could be going on to another assignment. At the end of the period, I collect the work of the students whose names remain on the list. (Carole Parent, teacher)

■ I don't go home to mark books and come back the next day, return them, and hope by the third day the corrections will get done. I'm able to give feedback to the students on the spot and this has given me a better handle on what their skills are. (Sonja Karsh, teacher)

Whenever possible, save paper and time by reviewing students' computer work on-screen, rather than having them print out all assignments. Assignments that focus on process more than product require a record of the students' having completed the work rather than a hard copy of the end product. A portfolio of daily work reflects progress over the long term. This might be a computer record (see Figure 8.4), notebook, tracking sheet with comments (see Chapter 6, page 92, Figure 6.10), unit of work, and/or representative samples selected in consultation with the student.

Figure 8.4

Using the type of computer record illustrated here, the teacher can see which practices or tests the student has completed, simply by selecting "Practice" or "Test." This screen indicates that the student has finished the lessons in each module.

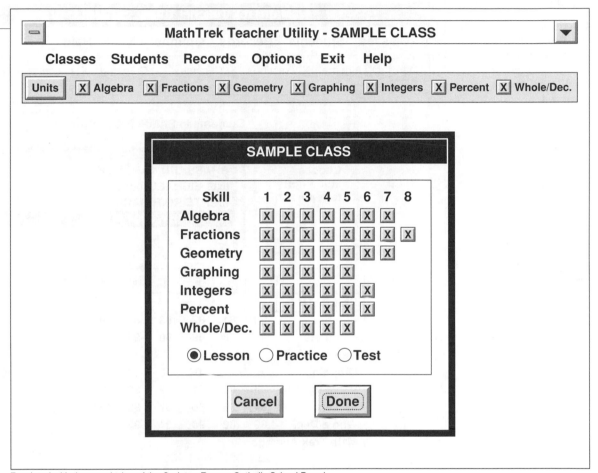

Reprinted with the permission of the Carleton Roman Catholic School Board

Tests

Some kinds of formal testing remain an important part of today's educational environment. Technology can improve this testing process. Software is now available that will help you to create, administer, and mark tests, and to record and organize student marks. Many test-creation packages draw randomly from a databank of items that test the same skill. This flexibility allows students to retake tests with ease as they move ahead toward mastery of specific skills and allows teachers to reuse the same test format many times. The tests can be used in both formative and summative ways.

■ A valuable characteristic of computers is that they are extremely good for providing students with continuous feedback. It is important for teachers to encourage students to make effective use of this feedback.[4]

Immediate feedback is one of the positive aspects of on-screen testing and students frequently want to go back and try again to improve their scores. The drawbacks to on-screen testing are the requirement of large numbers of computers for student access and the limitation of a question format. Computer-generated and -scored tests can include multiple-choice items, true and false, matching, and short-answer questions. Grade- or mark-management software is readily available.

Figure 8.5

Good computer-assisted instruction software includes the testing component as an integral part of the program.

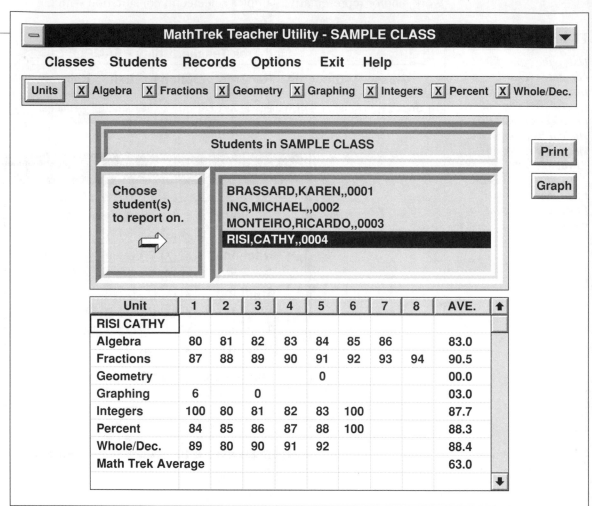

Unit	1	2	3	4	5	6	7	8	AVE.
RISI CATHY									
Algebra	80	81	82	83	84	85	86		83.0
Fractions	87	88	89	90	91	92	93	94	90.5
Geometry					0				00.0
Graphing	6		0						03.0
Integers	100	80	81	82	83	100			87.7
Percent	84	85	86	87	88	100			88.3
Whole/Dec.	89	80	90	91	92				88.4
Math Trek Average									63.0

Reprinted with the permission of the Carleton Roman Catholic School Board

Regardless of the fact that a test is computer-generated, -administered, and -scored, a test is only as good as its design. If you are responsible for designing a test, creating itcms, or evaluating a commercially prepared test, these guidelines may be helpful:

- Does the test focus on the highly specific learning outcomes that you have identified?
- Does each item really test what you want it to test ?
- Is each question clearly stated ?
- Are students completely familiar with the various types of questions used in the test?
- Are clear and helpful visual materials provided as required, in the form of text passages, graphs, and illustrations?
- Are students permitted to use reference materials and/or aids such as calculators or concrete materials where appropriate?

Figure 8.6

A variety of data is available to the student and teacher in post-test screens such as these.

- Is there ample time for each student to complete all questions?
- Can a student return to the test at another time in order to complete or recheck it?
- Do students understand the marking criteria and marking scheme?
- Can students rewrite in order to improve their marks?

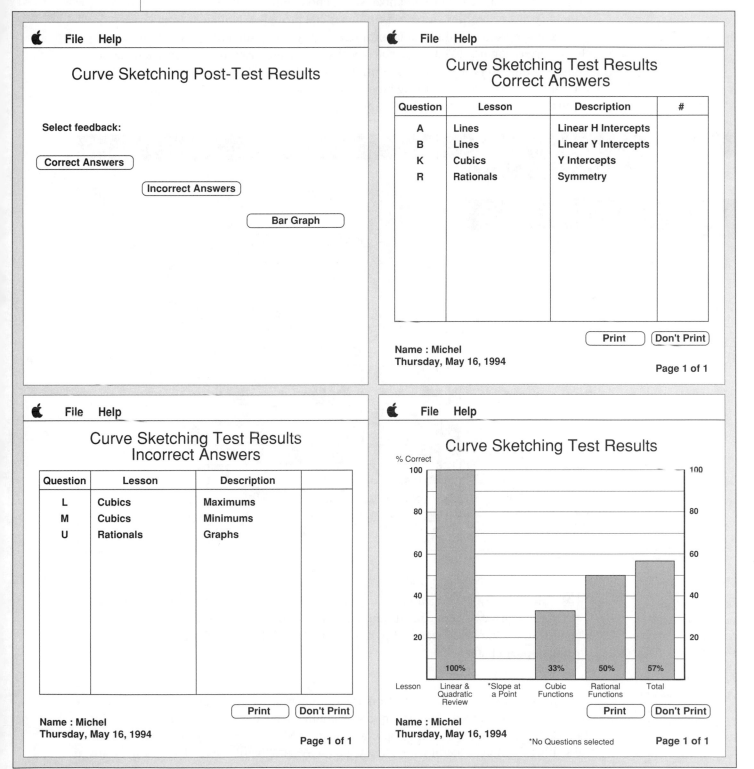

Reprinted with the permission of the Carleton Roman Catholic School Board

Portfolio assessment

It is difficult to manage the great volume and variety of evaluative information gathered on each student on an ongoing basis. You may end up with many files, folders, diaries, self-stick notes, videotapes, observation checklists, and more. Now, computer software can help organize, store, and communicate this information to parents. Student profiles stored on computer can provide sophisticated and easily accessed assessment of individual progress. All types of student work (writing, drawings, assignments) can be electronically stored and used for teaching and parent conferencing. You can enter these samples of student work from their personal disks, on a shared network, or by using an optical scanner. You can directly input data such as observations, test scores, and achievement of benchmarks, as shown in Figure 8.7.

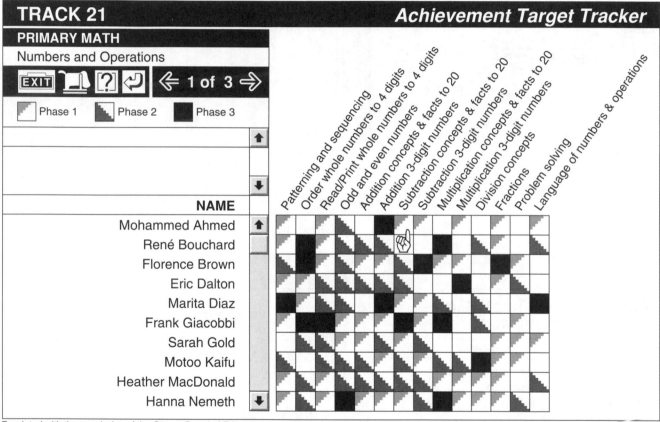

Reprinted with the permission of the Ottawa Board of Education

Figure 8.7

With the click of a mouse button, the teacher can indicate each student's degree of mastery of a benchmark. Records can follow a student from year to year. Updating is simple and efficient.

■ Most traditional educational systems will do better on traditional evaluations than innovative systems. Most innovations will not do any better than traditional education if they are measured by traditional tests. This is the Catch 22 in educational change.[5]

The tools available for evaluation are as numerous as the letters of the alphabet. As you think of ways in which technology could enhance or improve each evaluation method, record your ideas on a copy of Blackline Master 8.7. Because some items are subskills of a more general competency, you may find that the same technologies are sometimes repeated.

BLM 8.7

Tools for Evaluation

Evaluation Method	Technology
A - anecdotal records, at-a-glance sheets	
B - benchmarks	
C - conferencing, checklists	
D - drawings, diaries, daily work	
E - experiments	
F - folders of student work	
G - group work	
H - hearing what students are saying	
I - interviews	
J - journals	
K - knowledge appraisal	
L - listening, leadership	
M - marking, monitoring	
N - notes	
O - oral presentations	
P - presentations, projects	
Q - quizzes	
R - rating scales, responses	
S - skill development	
T - tests, tasks, time-lines	
U - understanding	
V - verbal communication	
W - written work	
X - (e)xaminations	
Y - yes! positive attitude	
Z - zeal/enthusiasm	

CHAPTER 9

Students with Special Needs

Laws requiring the least restrictive environment for children with special needs result in mainstreaming. Budget cuts cause reductions in programs for gifted and talented children. Whatever the reasons, many classroom teachers are becoming responsible for an ever-widening diversity of students, and they are not going to be able to meet the needs of these children without making some changes. Diverse needs are going to require the flexibility of diverse approaches in classrooms.[1]

Every class is made up of individuals, each with a preferred learning style. Some are highly visual learners, others work best through auditory channels, and still others learn well by moving around and manipulating real objects. The range of exceptional students integrated into any given classroom may include physically challenged, mentally handicapped, visually or auditorily impaired, learning disabled, intellectually gifted, attentional-deficit disordered, hyperactive, and various combinations of these. With the addition of increasing numbers of students for whom English is a second language, we see a complex puzzle of students with many different needs to be met within the context of one classroom.

As we search for ways to meet these varied needs, technology can provide invaluable assistance. Using technology can free the special student from a history of negative traditional learning experiences and can provide control and autonomy that may previously have been missing. Not only is technology highly motivating for most students, but it can be used to implement and complement the strategies that we already know are helpful in working with students with special needs. Each exceptionality is unique and thus requires specialized knowledge, techniques, and technologies. Rather than attempting to delve in detail into each exceptionality, we have chosen to examine, in general terms, some strategies that may be useful for many students with a range of special needs.

Using technology to individualize your program

Individualization of programs is no longer a sophisticated technique for the "master" teacher. Rather, it has become a necessity. True individualization includes adapting to individual needs for pacing, repetition, and the quantity and quality of the material being presented. Technology can help you to move toward your goal of creating and implementing a more individualized program.

> ■ I don't want this to sound like a cliché but it's really true. I have students who are gifted and have used the [technology-integrated] program. They have been able to work at their own levels. Other children who need additional reinforcement are also able to get that through the [technology-integrated] program. (Sonja Karsh, teacher)
>
> ■ If you are having difficulty, then you can stay at your own level. When you are just learning with the whole class, you go up to a higher level whether you understand it or not. (Student)

Computers, in particular, allow differentiated instruction for the special-needs student. Four basic principles for evaluation of computer software for special-needs students have been suggested:

- Use of computer technology must be appropriate. The computer is not always the best medium.
- Software must be compatible with learner needs and characteristics.
- Software must be compatible with the needs and intentions of the teacher.
- Software must be compatible with the curriculum.[2]

Resources that can easily be accessed and used with a minimum of assistance are of the greatest benefit. For students with learning difficulties, look for software that incorporates features such as:

- reduction of distraction and irrelevant stimuli;
- simplification and repetition of task directions;
- an abundance of practice;
- modeling and demonstrations;
- prompts and cues;
- instruction in small, manageable steps;
- immediate and frequent reinforcement and feedback.

For intellectually gifted students, look for software that incorporates features such as:

- open-ended questions;
- student-controlled choices and levels;
- content introduced in highly stimulating ways;
- immediate and frequent reinforcement and feedback.

Be aware that not all learners with the same condition will respond in the same way to the same software program — what works with one special-needs student may not work with another; thus, authorable software is of particular interest to teachers of special-needs students. Authorable software refers to software to which data such as individual spelling lists or stories can be entered. This allows you to customize activities for students. These kinds of easy modifications will assist the exceptional student to participate as a fully equal class member and to join with the other students in the regular daily program.

Use technology to do the job of introducing, teaching, or reinforcing skills to one group of students while you work with another group. While students are engaged in tasks using computers, videotapes, videodiscs, or audiotapes, you are free to conference and work with individuals on a one-to-one basis. A learning center/workstation approach is required to make this work well. Information on how to plan and establish workstations in your classroom can be found in Chapter 5, "What About Curriculum?" and Chapter 6, "Getting Started."

■ I have the time during class to focus on the abilities of my kids. I can sit with students right away, mark their book and focus on the area or objective where they are having difficulty. (Jim Rogers, teacher)

Figure 9.1

Plans laid out within a set format on the computer are easy to access and can be updated in a minute. Progress reports can be jotted onto the profile quickly and then elaborated on later when more time is available.

Planning for the exceptional student often requires an individual pupil program that sets out very specific learning goals for the student. These goals may be of an academic or a social/behavioral nature, as shown in Figure 9.1. Regardless of the type of goals, they require careful monitoring and tracking. This arduous task is greatly facilitated by using the computer. Select software that can assist in planning and tracking individualized educational programs. Once you get into the habit of using the computer for student record-keeping, you will never go back to the days of shuffling and filing endless sheets of paper.

Individualized Education Plan

SKILLS: Communication: __X__   Behavior: __X__

            Gross Motor: _____   Fine Motor: _____

Long-Term Goals	Short-Term Objectives	Methods/Strategies	Evaluation Methods	Progress Report Term 1
Decode short words with consonant-vowel-consonant (CVC) patterns	Short "a" words Short "i" words	Word families Patterning Autoskills reading	Decode random sample of 20 short "a" CVC words	Short "a": Score 18/20 Short "i": Score 17/20
Use context clues for predicting	Select an appropriate next word based on context of simple, familiar stories	Familiar stories Cloze passages (oral)	Miscue analysis	
On-task behavior	Work for five minutes with no intervention	Behavior modification using growth chart Daily reporting to home	Daily chart	

Technology can also provide evaluation that helps to individualize programs. Many computer programs include an evaluation component. In some programs, students move through modules in which mastery of certain skills or concepts is required before the student can progress to the next module. Because a computer can randomly generate questions based on a common format, students can practice a skill as often as is required for mastery. Once you know the computer program thoroughly yourself, you will know exactly what the student must understand in order to successfully complete the lesson or module. When you see evidence of that successful completion, you can be confident that the student has learned the skill.

A computer evaluation may also be diagnostic in nature and used as a basis for assigning appropriate follow-up learning activities, whether or not they are technology-oriented, as shown in Figures 9.2 (below) and 9.3 (on the next page). In the program shown in Figure 9.2, a computer test assigns activity cards at various levels of difficulty. Following completion of this test, each student receives a graphic profile of achievement. In this case, the unit focuses on measurement skills. Specific tasks are assigned to students according to their degree of mastery of each subskill in the test. Remedial and enrichment groups can also be easily established using this information.

Figure 9.2

A student bar graph from a measurement unit.

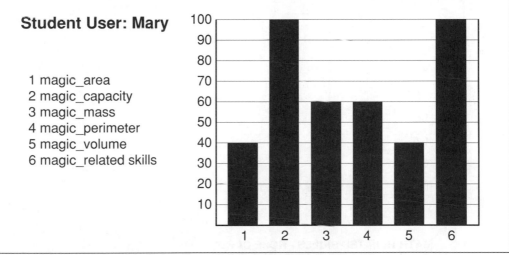

Reprinted with the permission of the Carleton Roman Catholic School Board

◼ The children are monitored constantly and they [teachers] can address the different skills, whether students need to be remediated or provided with an enrichment program in an area. That feedback comes from the program. (Bev Murphy, principal)

Another approach is for a school or school system to develop a bank of assessment items on a specific topic. These items are then put onto a computer disk or CD-ROM. When a teacher wants to test students' understanding of a particular skill, there are many items from which to choose. If a written test is appropriate, the selected items can be printed out. You may not yet have such resources in your school, but be alert for them as they come onto the marketplace. Remember that truly authentic assessment includes portfolios of student work, observational data, and performance appraisal. The techniques outlined in Chapter 8, "Evaluating Student Progress," are appropriate for all students, including those with special needs.

Figure 9.3

An individualized student tracking sheet such as this may be produced as an outcome of a test taken on the computer. In this example, the asterisked items are the mandatory assignments for this student.

Measurement Magic 4 Test

STUDENT: _____

ASSIGNMENT DATE	COMMENT	ASSIGNMENT DATE	COMMENT

MATH VIEWING - ORANGE CARDS

1A ☐ _____ _____
1B ☐ _____ _____
*1C ☐ _____ _____
2A ☐ _____ _____
*2B ☐ _____ _____
2C ☐ _____ _____
3A ☐ _____ _____
3B ☐ _____ _____
3C ☐ _____ _____
*4A ☐ _____ _____
4B ☐ _____ _____
4C ☐ _____ _____
5A ☐ _____ _____
*5B ☐ _____ _____
5C ☐ _____ _____
6A ☐ _____ _____
6B ☐ _____ _____
*6C ☐ _____ _____
7 ☐ _____ _____

MATH-RELATED SKILLS - ROSE CARDS

*1A ☐ _____ _____
1B ☐ _____ _____
1C ☐ _____ _____
2A ☐ _____ _____
*2B ☐ _____ _____
2C ☐ _____ _____
3A ☐ _____ _____
3B ☐ _____ _____
*3C ☐ _____ _____
4A ☐ _____ _____
4B ☐ _____ _____

MATH-RELATED SKILLS (cont.) - ROSE CARDS

4C ☐ _____ _____
5A ☐ _____ _____
*5B ☐ _____ _____
5C ☐ _____ _____
6A ☐ _____ _____
6B ☐ _____ _____
*6C ☐ _____ _____
*7A ☐ _____ _____
7B ☐ _____ _____
7C ☐ _____ _____
8 ☐ _____ _____

MATH PROBLEM SOLVING - PURPLE CARDS

1A ☐ _____ _____
*1B ☐ _____ _____
1C ☐ _____ _____
*2A ☐ _____ _____
2B ☐ _____ _____
2C ☐ _____ _____
3A ☐ _____ _____
3B ☐ _____ _____
*3C ☐ _____ _____
4A ☐ _____ _____
*4B ☐ _____ _____
4C ☐ _____ _____
5A ☐ _____ _____
5B ☐ _____ _____
*5C ☐ _____ _____
*6A ☐ _____ _____
6B ☐ _____ _____
6C ☐ _____ _____

Cooperative learning and peer helping

Research supports our experience that the strategy of students working in pairs on the computer is often more effective than students working individually.[3] This is particularly true when the activity is of a problem-solving nature, but does not always apply to drill and practice software, word processing, or keyboarding skills.

Students working in pairs have been observed to do better work, to be better able to solve their own problems without teacher intervention, and to be on-task more of the time than when working individually.[4]

■ Children who work together at a computer are routinely observed to correct each other's mistakes, cooperate in the completion of assigned tasks, and discuss the assignments in ways that clarify the task, even when neither partner appears to understand it at the outset. . . . Growing evidence suggests that collaboration at a machine reduces low-level errors and creates support for higher level activities.[5]

For students with special needs, providing a "buddy" often makes it possible for them to participate in the regular activities of the classroom. A buddy can help a physically disadvantaged student to manipulate equipment, read for a non-reader, check organization and completeness for a learning-disabled classmate, help a distractible partner to stay on-task, or communicate in the first language of a non-English-speaking friend. When faced with a particular student whose needs are very specific, the role of a buddy is easy to define.

Cooperative learning groups are another way to provide the support that the exceptional student often needs. A group of students can watch a video together, listen to an audiotape together, or work on an interactive computer program. The teacher's skill in facilitating cooperative learning and the students' teamwork skills are just as important when using computers as they are in any other cooperative learning activity.

Guidelines for group work, developed with the students, will help activities to run smoothly. When roles are carefully assigned to group members, each student has a chance to contribute in a meaningful way to the final product. For example, the gifted student can be given a more challenging role, such as facilitator, recorder, checker or questioner, whereas a less able student might fare best in a role such as materials manager, time-keeper, or noise monitor.

It is not always necessary for all students in a learning group to complete an identical activity. An assignment can be structured so that some students are expected to do the basics while other students receive enrichment. The cooperative part of the task is in the helping, editing, and checking. Self-esteem is enhanced and confidence will grow.

Telecommunications is yet another way to allow students to interface with each other and solve problems cooperatively. Gifted students in particular benefit from contact with the "real world" by the use of telecommunications to enhance their studies. For example, a student might contact a scientist to obtain information for a project, a peer at another school who has a similar interest, or an expert who could act as a mentor in developing a new skill.

Modifying your program

It is neither realistic nor desirable to strive for a classroom in which students work on individualized programs or in cooperative learning groups all of the time. Whole-class instruction remains an integral part of the learning process, and many students learn very well this way. A mix of approaches produces the best results. By modifying your program in some easy ways, you can enable the exceptional student to function as a competent class member in the whole-group setting.

Process

Modifying the process of your technology-integrated classroom might include modifying the physical setup of the classroom and also the daily routines. As mentioned in Chapter 6, "Getting Started," page 84, requirements for wheelchair access and a specific space design for physically or mentally challenged students should be taken into consideration. A laptop computer may be the best solution for a student whose mobility is severely restricted. For a highly distractible student, a single desk or study carrel may be required as a space for concentration when involved in an individual pursuit.

Some simple routines can make life much easier for exceptional students and save a lot of frustration. For example, before expecting students to complete a task individually, try doing one or more similar tasks as a whole group. These could result in sample pages of work in each notebook that remind students of your requirements (e.g., format, titles, organization). Show videos to the whole group and have some discussion before requiring students to look at them again for a specific purpose. When introducing new computer software, walk through it with the whole class before letting students explore on their own. These routines will benefit all students and are often lifesavers for certain exceptional students.

Color-coding of different workstations and/or activities is helpful to the learning-disabled, non-English-speaking, or mentally handicapped student who may otherwise have difficulty keeping track of movement and organizing work. You may need to break down some tasks into smaller steps or add more visual examples for certain students to be successful in working from written directions.

Figure 9.4

Highlighting key words on an activity card can help a special-needs student to easily understand instructions. When you make cards using a word processing program, simply bold, underline, box, change the font, or change the size of the most important words.

Center: Math Computation
Card: 2A

Hanging Around with Professor Perimeter

Professor Perimeter loves her work. She reminds you of the following.

> **Perimeter** is the distance around an object.
> To find **perimeter**, add all of the sides.

A. *Find* the **perimeter** of the figures below.

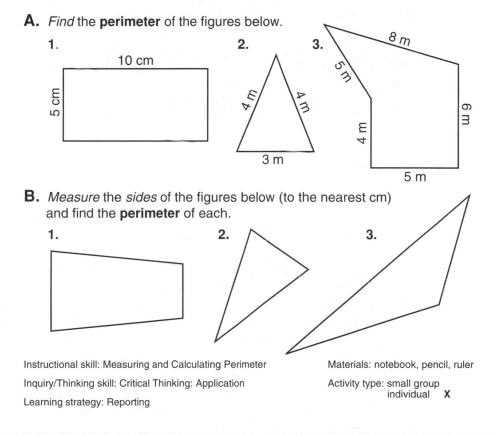

B. *Measure* the *sides* of the figures below (to the nearest cm) and find the **perimeter** of each.

Instructional skill: Measuring and Calculating Perimeter

Inquiry/Thinking skill: Critical Thinking: Application

Learning strategy: Reporting

Materials: notebook, pencil, ruler

Activity type: small group
individual   **X**

Reprinted with the permission of the Carleton Roman Catholic School Board

■ Use of the computers proves especially helpful to the children because the computers give them control over their own learning. On the one hand, the computer is very calm and patient with children who need different amounts of time to learn a word, read a sentence, or identify a picture. On the other hand, the computer is tremendously dynamic — the children get very excited by the voices, music and sound effects the computer adds to a story.[6]

Audiotapes of reading selections are often necessary for the student with reading difficulties. They allow the student to listen and read along. Conversely, a written copy of listening activities may be required for a hearing-impaired or non-English-speaking student. When teaching intellectually challenged students to use technology, avoid the use of highly technical terms, provide visual cues to accompany your auditory presentation, and allow time for lots of hands-on practice. Post a list of operating instructions at each piece of equipment for reference (see Chapter 6, "Getting Started," page 88, Figure 6.8). By providing a relaxed, comfortable learning environment, you enable all of your students to feel secure and you encourage risk-taking.

Content

For some special-needs students, the content of your program may be difficult. This is an area in which technology can be very useful. Look for computer programs that are self-paced, allow the student to work slowly in small steps, and provide instant feedback. Many software packages are available that have these features, especially in mathematics.

> ■ There is evidence that increased academic challenge (which can be facilitated by computers) is engaging for students with special needs. Seeing students "motivated and guided by well-chosen software, [teachers] expand their expectations for special needs students."[7]

In reading, on-screen storybooks with sound are wonderful for reluctant readers. These may be purchased on CD-ROM and often include a built-in dictionary or glossary. For younger students, this dictionary may be in the form of pictures. For example, the student highlights the word "doctor" on the computer screen and a picture of a doctor is shown. These are also a great resource for students for whom English is a second language.

The multimedia nature of CD-ROM and videodisc technology is especially beneficial in the presentation of abstract ideas. Many science concepts that are difficult to explain can be presented in a way that makes them easy to understand through electronic media. Magnetism is a good example. If you have ever tried to explain to students how atoms become aligned in a magnetized needle, with like poles facing the same way, you will appreciate the ease with which this can be done on a well-produced videodisc or electronic encyclopedia. Many electronic encyclopedias on CD-ROM also have charts, film clips, and graphics that help students to understand content. All learners, not just the learning disabled, benefit from the enhanced multisensory characteristics of multimedia.

> ■ The teaching characteristics of multimedia — the integration of video, audio, text and graphics — match the learning needs of students with learning disabilities.[8]

Product

Sometimes, you may be expecting a significantly different product from the special-needs student than from the rest of your students, because the learning goal for this student is completely different. In many cases, however, special-needs students can use the same materials and produce a final product that is appropriate for their levels of ability. The following strategies help in setting attainable standards for students with special needs, whether or not they are involved with technology:

- Reduce the number of workstations by eliminating those that are inappropriate, according to the student's individual tracking sheet.
- Reduce the number of questions given on an assignment card.
- Provide more structure by giving the student a prepared answer sheet (e.g., fill in the blanks).
- Allow the student to use a calculator, computer, or concrete materials whenever required.
- Allow the student to respond on audiocassette rather than in writing.
- Ask for pictures or diagrams instead of language.
- Conference with the student to allow for oral response instead of written.
- Give the student a small amount to do at one time and set a suitable time frame within which you expect it to be done.

Word processing is a terrific benefit for any student who has great difficulty with handwriting. With spell check and grammar check, these students can produce a neat, correct, final product.

■ Computers can become effective tools for raising self-esteem. Students who have met with repeated failures in their academic lives may find the objective non-human responses that they receive less threatening.[9]

Adaptive devices for special-needs students

The potential of technology to assist students with a variety of exceptionalities is virtually unlimited. Although it is likely that resource people within your school system (special education teachers, consultants, etc.) and the parents of the child will be the decision makers in this regard, be aware of some of the possibilities that technology allows.

Alternative input devices

Some students have difficulty or are unable to input into the computer with a keyboard, trackball, or mouse. Devices presently available to assist these students include:

- computers that operate through voice recognition;
- joysticks, paddles, and switches that are operated with the hand, foot, chin, or the raising of an eyebrow;
- keyguards, which are flat boards with finger holes that fit over the standard keyboard to stabilize hands and prevent accidental contact with the keys;

- plastic keyboard overlays that fit over the entire keyboard, allowing for temporary labeling or color-coding and protecting from spills or drooling;
- miniature keyboards requiring very little movement or force;
- king-sized keyboards that are less sensitive to touch, so that students cannot accidentally hit several keys at a time if they have spasms;
- power pads that are touch-sensitive, used instead of a keyboard;
- touch-sensitive programmable membrane boards that can be applied to the monitor to allow it to be used as a touch screen;
- keyboards that have keys representing sounds rather than letters;
- head control devices;
- voice input systems;
- scanners that scan text, visuals, and three-dimensional objects from outside sources into the computer;
- braille computers.

These are only some of the wide variety of alternative input devices that allow a special-needs student to participate in regular classroom activities and to optimize individual competencies.

■ All children will learn: not on the same day; not in the same way.[10]

Alternative output devices

Traditional methods of receiving output from the computer can also be a problem for some students. Again, new developments in technology can assist these students. Some of these include:

- magnified video display screens for use with video playback or computer;
- speech synthesizers allowing for audio output;
- braille output devices.

Technology has the potential to help teachers better meet student needs by allowing individual students to learn in their preferred ways. As technology advances and school systems find more ways to use technology, the hope is that it will become a tool that can give all students opportunities to succeed, not only in school, but also in future work and in life itself.

■ The one common thread in successful programs for the at-risk is individual attention. Fortunately, the technological tools necessary to provide individualization are readily available, but teachers must have access to and must implement the technology in their classrooms.[11]

CHAPTER 10

Tools for Teachers

...computers should be used by teachers to write lesson plans, reports, handouts, notes to students and teachers; to comment on student written work and other forms of expression; to keep track of student progress in their classroom activities; to facilitate classroom presentations and demonstrations; to keep up with professional developments and share ideas with colleagues, etc.[1]

It is wonderful to see your students motivated and excited by the power of technology. Now, what about you, the teacher? It is time for you to have a computer on your desk, too! Many schools and districts have initiated a "computer on every desk" program and many teachers have bought their own computers. All too frequently, however, technology is still placed only in the hands of students, while teachers are forgotten and the importance of leading by example is ignored.[2]

Just as students using technology are more motivated by tasks and exhibit more care in their final products, so technology has the power to energize teachers, increase their productivity, create pride in their accomplishments, and renew the challenge of teaching. Furthermore, computer use is associated with professionalism in our society: facility in using a computer has become one of the marks of an educated person.

Computer proficiency is essential for teachers, and they need initial training unless they enter the profession with some background in computer use. Also, as the technology changes and as new theories emerge regarding the role of technology in learning, continuing on-the-job training is important. Most teachers want to use technology and see that technology holds potential for them, but many need encouragement to invest the time required for the change. They realize that the very opportunities afforded by the computer initially make tasks more difficult and time-consuming. Nonetheless, computer literacy is an investment that will pay off handsomely in the long run.

This chapter points out some ways in which using a computer can make you more productive, more creative, and more flexible in your profession. Computer use is examined for lesson planning and presentation, teacher utilities, telecommunicating, and administrative tasks.

■ If computer technology is to have an impact on teaching and learning, teachers must be comfortable with computers, seeing them as tools that enhance rather than interfere with their daily teaching. For this to happen, teachers need special training.[3]

By substituting an overhead projector and LCD panel for the chalkboard, you can prepare a lesson before the class on the computer, store it, and reuse it from class to class or in subsequent years. The quality of the presentation is better than from the chalkboard, it is quickly and easily modifiable, and the whole class can share a single computer without crowding around a small monitor.

Lesson planning and presentation

Both long- and short-term planning are best done using a flexible tool that allows easy editing and modification, because timetables, unit plans, weekly schedules, and daily plans are all susceptible to interference by unscheduled interruptions and special events.

Once you have set up a suitable daily or weekly planning format on computer, you can enter events and activities quickly and make any required changes easily. If you are fortunate enough to have a computer on your desk, there is no need to print out a paper copy. Even if you have to share a computer with your students, it is still more efficient to enter and print out your next day's plans than to write them by hand, once you become used to doing this. Try a variety of formats until you find one that best suits your needs (see examples in Chapter 6, "Getting Started," Figures 6.4 through 6.6, pages 85-86).

Use of the computer also facilitates the production of quality lessons in less time. Some lessons are best presented directly from the computer, for example, using a

spreadsheet to demonstrate number patterns in mathematics, a graphics program to demonstrate the effect of color on mood, or a computer-assisted learning module to introduce a new skill. An LCD (liquid crystal display) tablet used on an overhead projector, for example, allows projection from the computer onto a large screen for whole-class lessons. From formal presentations to the generation of samples of creative writing or math equations, more useful material can be created in less time using a computer.

■ . . . once teachers are competent "productivity tool" users, they frequently search for ways to use these same computer powers to enhance their classroom instruction.[4]

Multimedia is an exciting way to create classroom presentations and some lessons lend themselves well to the diversity that multimedia makes possible. However, we would caution the new user that the process of creating a multimedia lesson is labor-intensive and requires careful planning and some technical expertise. The benefit of creating a multimedia presentation is that once you have invested the initial time into its creation, you have a product you can use many times over.

■ Depending on their style, some teachers teach themselves multimedia; others learn it from their fellow teachers or from their students. Teachers who are successful find ways to use multimedia personally to:

- make presentations
- transform textbook materials into a multimedia format
- conduct original research
- bring new life to "tired" knowledge
- renew their commitment to teaching.[5]

If you feel ready to tackle the challenge of creating a multimedia lesson presentation, try using the following steps as a guideline:

- Identify a specific content area.
- Have a clear understanding of what the students will be able to do at the end of the lesson.
- Develop an outline to organize and sequence content.
- Create a checklist of appropriate media materials for inclusion.
- Consider a variety of presentation methods.
- Create a storyboard.
- Produce the lesson.[6]

Student handouts and worksheets created on the computer can be cleaner, sharper, and more interesting than those produced by hand. Graphics are easily added and often make assignments more appealing to younger students.

Teacher utilities

Software designed specifically to facilitate everyday teacher tasks is now readily available (e.g., puzzle-generating software). Teachers often use various types of puzzles to reinforce vocabulary, provide spelling practice, or develop thinking skills. With a puzzle generator, crossword puzzles and word searches are quick and easy to develop. Students can also use this software to make puzzles for their classmates.

Text or reading-level analysis programs are available that evaluate the reading level of passages of text. This type of program would probably be a useful tool for selecting appropriate student reading materials from magazines, newspapers, and textbooks.

■ . . . too often, labs were underused, or, worse, became a haven for computer-game playing. The problem, it came to be seen, was that no one had instructed teachers about how computers can be used to teach the curriculum and, perhaps more importantly, the teachers themselves did not have access to a computer.[7]

The assessment and evaluation tools described in Chapter 8, " Evaluating Student Progress," might also be considered teacher utilities, particularly test-generating software, which either provides databanks of items from which to choose or allows you to create your own items. The test can be printed out and duplicated for student use. Some testing packages enable students to take the test on-screen and, on completion, the computer marks responses and provides immediate results. These results are then compiled for teacher access — saving a lot of valuable time.

Multimedia portfolios have exciting potential at all levels and in all subject areas. New multimedia software allows teachers to compare student work to school or system standards (actual samples are scanned into the document or video clips are inserted). Teachers can record individual student progress, cross-reference each benchmark to related resources, and print out reports for parents — all at the touch of a button.

Telecommunications

Many new schools are cabled for internal electronic mail (e-mail), allowing instant communication with other classes, teachers, and office staff. This conserves time previously spent tracking down busy colleagues to convey simple messages. Administrative and professional tasks can also be greatly facilitated when e-mail links the school to the outside world (e.g., schools are often linked to one another and/or their central office buildings). In the past, trying to reach another teacher during school hours often involved the frustration of hearing, "He's on yard duty right now" or "She's coaching a soccer practice for the next hour." With telecommunications, you can leave a message that you are sure the other person will receive.

■ One of the biggest thorns in teaching is communicating with other faculty members, because everyone is on a different schedule. With . . . electronic mail, however, we've found it much easier to communicate with one another because we can send and receive messages whenever it's convenient. Even better, we use electronic mail for collaborating — to share lesson plans, student data, and other resources.[8]

Telecommunications can link you to other teachers, to a researcher at a university, or to experts in the community. Picture yourself participating in an on-line conference about using new software, in which you can share your own thoughts as well as read those of others. After the conference ends, you can "call up" your new contacts to exchange worksheets and lessons. In these days of diminishing resources in education, the ability to conference, consult, collaborate, and share with peers efficiently is increasingly important.

■ . . . the soul of a Free-Net lies in the people who use it and are free to create as many uses for it as their imagination will allow.[9]

Not only do a modem, a telephone line, and connection to a network provide access to human resources, they also provide access to constantly updated databases of information. With a short time investment, you can do just about any type of research required for presentations or lesson planning.

Administrative tasks

Computer use can expedite administrative tasks, thus giving you more time to teach. A wise choice of software for beginners is an integrated package containing several software programs that allow easy movement from program to program. A typical combination might include word processing, a database, a spreadsheet, graphics, and telecommunications.

Word processing software can be used for a variety of administrative purposes, including:

- newsletters;
- invitations;
- signs and posters;
- memos to students and/or colleagues;
- test creation;
- seating plans;
- letters to parents;
- permission forms for trips.

All of these can be tailored to suit the specific event, modified as often as you want, and saved for use in following months and years. As an example of how a computer can make your communications with parents more direct and professional, personalizing letters is easy using the mail-merge feature of a word processor. Simply identify the variable part of your letter (e.g., name and address), create a list of the variable information, and print out the letters, with the computer changing the variable information each time.

A database is the easiest way to keep track of a variety of student information, such as names, addresses, telephone numbers, birth dates, names of parents/guardians, bus routes, immunizations, and emergency information (see Figure 10.1). Your school secretary may already have this information, which could be passed on to you on a disk. If not, it may take a couple of hours for you to enter this data, but the subsequent ability to sort, modify, access, and print specific information as required makes the initial work most worthwhile. A database could also be useful for keeping inventories of textbooks or classroom supplies.

Name	Birth Date	Address	Parent(s)/Guardian(s)	Telephone Numbers	Health Information
Armano, Mari	3/12/80	35 Appian Way	Roberto & Maria Armano	236-5786/562-6712	bee-sting allergy use epi-pen
Beare, Ron	27/06/81	4678 Nelson St.	Janet Beare	820-8463	
Cyr, Guy	16/04/80	786 Rice Ave. #1284	Simone Lefebvre & André Cyr	469-3209/469-0098 836-4766 (grandmother)	glasses
Fong, Loy	31/10/82	566 Main St.	Norman & Emi Fong	829-6938/567-8770 256-7221	

Figure 10.1

Once you have created a student database, information gathering is simple. For example, when asked for the names of students falling into a particular age range, it takes only a moment to sort and print the required list.

■ The important point to be made is the virtually instantaneous retrieval of data and the ability to pass that data on to somebody else with a minimum of effort. Once you have such a system [class database]...you will not ever want to go back to the old way.[10]

A spreadsheet can be used to maintain a budget, whether for classroom supplies, fund-raising events, a milk program, or a class trip. It can save hours of work. Spreadsheets are commonly used to keep track of marks or grades because they make it easy to total scores and find averages, as illustrated in Figure 10.2 on the next page.

Figure 10.2

With a spreadsheet, you can see the results of individual assignments as well as the cumulative marks and averages.

Mark Sheet: Class 6E

Student	Test	Test	Test	Test	Test	Notebook	Assignment 1	Assignment 2	Assignment 3	Project	Exam	Total	Average
	10	10	10	10	10	20	30	20	20	20	40	200	
Date	18-Oct	22-Oct	27-Oct	1-Nov	5-Nov	12-Nov	19-Nov	25-Nov	8-Dec	15-Dec	18-Dec		
Armano, Mari	8	6	7	7	6	17	23	18	19	17	38	166	83
Atkinson, Jennifer	6	7	5	6	7	18	24	18	18	16	35	160	80
Beare, Ron	Ab.	5	6	7	6	19	26	19	16	17	28		78
Bernetti, Steve	8	8	8	7	7	20	25	17	18	15	25	158	79
Chavez, Anita	9	10	9	8	9	19	27	16	17	18	32	174	87
Chenier, Marc	5	6	6	7	7	17	19	15	15	14	Ab.		69
Cyr, Guy	10	8	9	8	8	16	28	19	16	17	35	174	87
Davis, Shauna	9	8	7	7	6	15	28	18	19	18	38	173	87
Erasmus, Keetah	8	7	8	6	7	17	27	19	17	15	36	167	84
Fong, Loy	8	8	7	7	8	18	25	16	18	14	33	162	81
Hayward, Dayna	5	9	9	6	8	16	28	18	15	17	38	169	85
Jakowski, Irene	6	6	7	7	5	18	28	17	12	12	22	140	70
Lopez, Ramon	4	4	8	6	7	17	22	15	10	13	18	124	62
McKye, Kyle	6	7	5	Ab.	6	19	28	18	13	15	30		76
McLean, Robert	7	8	6	7	7	16	26	17	19	16	26	155	78
Marachin, Carl	9	9	9	8	9	15	24	16	14	15	25	153	77
Nishimura, Katie	10	10	8	7	6	17	26	17	15	17	30	163	82
Nisbet, Kathy	8	7	6	7	8	15	27	19	11	12	22	142	71
Olsgaard, Jim	7	6	7	6	8	19	29	20	18	19	40	179	90
Schlattmann, Jon	9	5	7	8	7	18	28	18	16	16	32	164	82
Sidorova, Erika	8	9	8	7	7	15	27	17	17	14	28	157	79
Stafford, Cindy	7	10	10	8	8	17	29	19	17	16	20	161	81
Williams, Brenda	5	8	7	7	6	16	25	16	15	11	26	142	71
											Class Average		79

Commercially available gradebook software allows you to input marks, assign differential weighting for various tests and assignments, and immediately see the final results. Students can be sorted alphabetically or by grade, and space is often provided for teacher comments. Spreadsheets are also useful for tracking student attendance. You can buy software for attendance that allows you to record student names, enter the times absent or late, and then do a variety of searches (e.g., by name, date, homeroom class). Using an integrated package, you can import student names from your database into various spreadsheets, thus saving time.

To obtain exactly the format that you want, you might prefer to design your own scoring or attendance sheet. You can also use a spreadsheet for keeping track of inventory: serial numbers of equipment, items that are out for repair, things borrowed and returned by students.

Figure 10.3

A computer appointment book is useful for keeping track of meetings, dates, and notes. A quick glance at the beginning of each day can help you to organize time most efficiently.

My Daily Planner		
Date November 23		

	Appointment/Task	Completed
7:00		
7:30		
8:00	Meeting with Mrs. Murray in vice-principal's office	✓
8:30	Consult with principal, Mrs. Zanon	
9:00		
9:30		
10:00		
10:30		
11:00	Phone Shauna's social worker	✓
11:30	Meet with the school psychologist	✓
12:00		
12:30		
1:00		
1:30		
2:00		
2:30		
3:00		
3:30	Workshop on networking — conference room	✓
4:00		
4:30		
5:00		
5:30		
6:00		
6:30		

To Do List	Notes
Prepare article for newsletter.	Speak to principal tomorrow.

Figure 10.4

Imagine how many activities in your week might be different when using technology. This is an example of a week's technology-related accomplishments of a teacher of 9- to 14-year-olds.

TEACHER'S TECHNOLOGY-RELATED ACCOMPLISHMENTS

Monday
- Brought in disk of student handouts prepared at home on the weekend and printed them.
- Printed John's individual portfolio to prepare for a parent interview.
- Helped a group of students find information on the network for their theme project.
- In the evening, created a math test using a new software package and wrote a letter to a parent.

Tuesday
- Connected with a colleague overseas via electronic mail.
- Updated class spreadsheet (money saved for our trip) to reflect last week's fund-raiser.
- Supervised students as they completed the on-screen math test. Analyzed class results after school.

Wednesday
- Printed out individual test results and gave to students.
- Used the LCD tablet to present a lesson modified from last year.
- In the evening, made a crossword puzzle for student review of science vocabulary.

Thursday
- Used a database to prepare video order for next month and faxed it to the Media Center.
- Helped groups of students to prepare their multimedia projects based on our theme.
- In the evening made a quiz on the computer, cutting and pasting questions from old exams. Made some initial contacts with scientists on the network to get information in preparation for our next theme.

Friday
- Used desktop publishing to create a parent newsletter.
- Created banners for bulletin boards for next week's thematic unit.
- Found a reference for an article that a friend has been wanting and sent it e-mail.

Training

A common response from teachers when they hear about all of these possibilities is "This sounds great, but I don't know much about using technology. Where, when, and how do I go about learning to do all these things?" Start by examining the opportunities in your locale. Once you are committed to becoming technology-literate, look for mentors among your colleagues and for courses at local software companies, high schools, community colleges, and universities. Training in specific software is often available in the form of day-long seminars or evening classes of short duration.

■ Teachers traditionally look to universities to update and upgrade their teaching skills. In the case of computer skills, however, adult education courses offered by local high schools are often the most practical way to learn how to use specific software to improve productivity.

Sometimes the most efficient way to learn a piece of software is to first have an experienced user walk you through it, devote some time to personal experimentation and practice, and then meet again with the "expert" for clarification and problem solving. There is no substitute for hands-on experience when learning new software: jump in and tackle a task, keep the user's manual handy as a reference tool, and be prepared to confront some frustration.

If integration of technology into the curriculum is a goal in your school system, it is likely that some training and support will be offered to teachers. For example, there may be workshops with the following themes:

- the rationale underlying technology in education;
- learning to use specific equipment;
- resources in the form of computer software, CD-ROM, videodisc, etc., that are available to teachers;
- how to enhance effective teaching and learning strategies with technology;
- how to integrate technology into your curriculum;
- experienced teachers presenting successful classroom strategies;
- sharing experiences with peers;
- meeting the needs of every learner by individualizing.

Look for this type of practical assistance wherever you can find it. Conferences such as those of the International Society for Technology in Education (ISTE), the National Education Computing Conference (NECC), and the Educational Computing Organization of Ontario (ECOO) offer a variety of sessions for both beginners and experienced technology users. Both the workshops and resource displays at these conferences are very useful.

Journals are also great for keeping in touch with the latest technologies and teaching ideas. Encourage your principal or librarian to invest in a school subscription to magazines such as *Computers in Education, The Computing Teacher, Electronic Learning, Teaching and Computers,* and *Technology and Learning.*

Of course, all of these suggestions require a time commitment, so first explore the professional development opportunities in your school or school system. Quite often, money is set aside to free teachers from classroom duties for professional growth.

■ In the case of our schools, the teacher is trained in the instruction delivery methods which were in use two centuries ago. The technology — a chalk and chalkboard — is at a 19th century level. . . . Teachers need to be afforded an opportunity to enhance their productivity, give their students the benefits that the most sophisticated instruction delivery systems offer, make an impact on hitherto insoluble educational problems, and bring education into the 21st century on an equal footing with business and government in using the advanced technologies which we have devised.[11]

If your school or school system administration is not helpful in the move to integrate technology, you can still pursue your personal goals. Contact colleagues in other schools and districts to find a support group. Try expressing your interest in educational technology on a telecommunications network: you may meet a community of people with a common interest. Utilize parent help, both for working with students and helping you to learn new software. Look for conference funding through professional associations and service organizations, and actively pursue assistance from the local business community through connections such as friends and parents. By sharing your enthusiasm with others, you may start a movement capable of creating change.

In Chapter 1, "Why Integrate Technology into the Classroom?" we cited lifelong learning as an essential skill in today's world. Lifelong learning means staying up to date by whatever means available.

■ Continuous personal and professional development is the minimum requirement for success today. . . . If you're not adding to your store of knowledge aggressively and continuously, you're actually falling behind.[12]

By assessing the contemporary technological skills required and consciously directing your natural abilities toward the development of these skills, you can become a technological teacher. Set a realistic personal technology goal, such as learning to use one new piece of software each term, and be prepared to use some evenings, a few hours each weekend, and/or holiday time to accomplish it. Remember to document your personal growth as you go along, so that your résumé will reflect the personal initiative you have demonstrated.

■ Each person is the president of [his or her] own career. As the president of ME Inc., you have to set up your own training department.[13]

If you're a novice, keep these tips in mind as you go through the learning process:

• It can be done.
• It's exciting, fun, and easy to use a computer.
• Don't be afraid — it won't break.
• Learning to use new hardware or new software can be difficult and frustrating at first, but it's always worth the trouble.
• Hang in there — the best is yet to come.
• No one is an expert.
• You can't learn it all in one day
• You will never know it all.[14]

Toward the Future

The best way to predict the future is to invent it.[1]

Technology has changed the world, our lives, and our students' lives — but this is only the beginning. Knowledge will continue to explode and increase in complexity at a tremendous speed. Already, with a few quick clicks of a mouse, we can hook into an ever-expanding information superhighway system that connects millions of people and thousands of universities, businesses, museums, and government offices around the world. Accurate and up-to-date information is at our fingertips. Telecommunications technologies are bringing interactive courses into remote locations and allowing students and teachers to participate in cooperative learning at a distance.

Technology is taking us into cyberspace and virtual worlds. We can electronically tour the Louvre, land an aircraft, walk in a foreign country, or join others in a collaborative adventure game. The whole world can become your "virtual classroom." How can you address these constantly changing new realities? You can embrace change for the excitement and challenges it brings, become a lifelong learner yourself, and move from contemplating the here and now to strategic planning for the future.

■ A NEW PARADIGM OF EDUCATION
- educator as futurist — facilitator, guide
- permanent white water of change — surf's up
- accept holistic, inter-disciplinary, process-oriented curriculum, global in nature not atomized bits
- place pedagogy before technology[2]

Celebrate your technological successes and share your stories with others. Once you become an agent of change yourself, you can inspire others to reflect on present practices, question the future, and take charge of change themselves in a proactive manner. Try using one or more of these questions as discussion-starters with colleagues, students, parents, school administrators, and friends.

- What are the basic skills required for the nineties and beyond?
- Will integration of technology simply allow schools to cover the same curricula faster or in more depth, or will it lead to the development of new and different curricula?

- How will student access to computer features such as spell check, grammar check, and punctuation check change the way spelling, grammar, and punctuation are taught in schools?
- Should the use of laptop computers in place of notebooks be banned because not all students can afford them? If computers and software are used to replace textbooks, how will this affect the allocation of funds for all educational resources?
- How will the role of the teacher change when students have access to massive amounts of information through telecommunications?
- When students have information at their fingertips, what methods of evaluation are appropriate?
- How will student presentations and projects change when multimedia workstations are readily available? What copyright issues will need to be addressed?
- If students are allowed to do their homework on computers, what must be done for the student who does not have a computer? How can sharing of computers and access to school computers be facilitated?
- Will the individualization of programs enabled by technology lead to schools without traditional grades?
- How will distance education change the school day and school year?
- What impact will computer voice recognition have on the teaching of language arts skills?
- What will "virtual reality" do for the learning of your students, when they can visit other worlds without leaving the classroom?
- As telecommunications reduces the barriers of geographical distance and links people to vast information resources, how will traditional organizations such as schools and school boards be affected?

■ This little essay asks you to turn your world on its head — to forget all the new technologies and instead turn your attention and your passion on your students. They are your salvation. The technologies are not important. Close your eyes and they will change. Blink and they will change again. They are transitory. Rather than see them as mobile Berlin "walls" that are rolled into your classroom, preventing you from seeing your own future, forget them. Repurpose these boxes and wires into sustenance for your students' minds. Let your students tackle the hardest, the most promising new technologies, and push your students to master these technologies. Percolate their knowledge around your classroom, and use the technologies to open new windows on content, on your curriculum, and your lessons that you never dreamed possible.[3]

Teachers and Technological Change

Figure 2.2 on page 19 in Chapter 2, "Where Are You Going?" diagrammatically describes the stages of change. Try to imagine yourself experiencing this journey of change. What will your actions be at each stage and how will you feel? We have probed and questioned, watched, listened to, and discussed this with many teachers of technology-integrated classrooms in all stages of implementation. We asked some teachers who are making change now to share their thoughts and feelings with us. They vary in their teaching experience and comfort level with technology, but they are all learning the important skill of adaptability. They are in control of change rather than having it imposed on them.

Awareness

Awareness is the first stage of change. Your professional reading, attendance at conferences, discussions with peers, and visits to other schools tell you that technological literacy is important and that technology can improve and revitalize the learning environment of a classroom. You would like to teach thematically and realize the benefits that large blocks of time hold for your students. Cooperative and individualized learning may be new to you, but you are eager to try out some of the strategies to which you have been exposed. You are aware of technology-enhanced programs but have not yet tried to use technology to any great extent in your classroom.

> *A Teacher's Diary*
>
> *Today I went to a workshop focusing on curriculum that involves technology. To tell you the truth, I'm a little frightened. I don't know a lot about technology and it sounds less structured than the way I'm used to running my classroom. I feel like I have good discipline and I'm not sure I can accept all the talking and activity. I think that the students will like it, though. It does seem more individualized and I like the way cooperative learning develops naturally.*

At this stage, try to articulate your vision of the technological classroom by identifying desired goals. Be sure that your goals are possible and you are not setting your sights so high that you are likely to fail. Ask yourself how you would like to grow in knowledge and expertise and how you can obtain training in the use of specific technologies. Consider, also, where your students are coming from. What experience do they have in working with technology? Are they experienced in the use of workstations? Have they had the opportunity to be involved in cooperative learning activities? Are they good independent learners? These factors will influence the goals that you establish for your classroom. Realizing that you will require support, think of the people who will be working with you and how to involve them. Formulate an action plan, seek the resources you will need, and decide how you will evaluate your plan.

A Teacher's Diary

I am finding out more about how to integrate technology into my classroom. In thinking about it, I feel like I'm on a roller coaster: I feel apprehensive at times, confused at other times, and sometimes confident that I can really do it. I guess I'm going to have to become a risk-taker.

Orientation

You have planned your change carefully, with attention to small details, and now feel ready to take some action. Remember that changes, particularly large ones, occur gradually.[1] You may feel pressure at this point and this is not unusual. Take advantage of any workshops and in-service training that will provide you with knowledge and resources.

A Teacher's Diary

I'm about to start my first technology-integrated unit. I'm feeling overwhelmed by the details of grouping, tracking, marking, and learning how to operate and care for the equipment. At the same time. I'm excited and eager, just like the kids.

Start slowly. Initially, you may develop one theme-related unit that focuses on specific skills. Incorporate some or all of the technological resources that you have on hand. Begin with whole-group learning if that is where you are most comfortable. Try some small-group and individual activities with your students. As you implement these activities, think of the different ways in which you are addressing the learning needs of your students.

A Teacher's Diary

I'm exhausted! It has taken many hours to get ready. I made extra copies of the audio- and videotapes so the kids won't fight over them. I gave each student a blank tape for speaking activities. I introduced all of the computer software during my computer lab time over the last few weeks. I've tested all of the students on the mastery skills I designated for the unit. I've introduced all of the workstations, we've done some sample activities as a whole group, and the walls are covered with charts, instructions for equipment, and reminders. Tomorrow, when we begin to work on individual and group projects, I'm sure I'll find out all of the small things that I didn't anticipate!

When you have completed that first unit, sit back and reflect on what occurred and what you would do differently next time. This is the ideal time to talk to a teacher who has been through the same process. At this point, the change still feels like a special project — it is still the exception and not the rule in your classroom.

> ## A Teacher's Diary
> I soon discovered that cooperating was not my students' strong point. It seemed like I was always having to intervene and solve group problems. I spoke to Marg about my cooperative learning problems. She has more experience in this and shared some techniques with me. I'm planning to take a course in cooperative learning next summer, but in the meantime I'll just muddle along as best I can.

Full implementation

Individuals vary in the amount of time it takes to progress to the stage of full implementation: it could be a few weeks, months, a year, or a few years. In fact, it is not unusual to take a step backward to evaluate and modify and then move on. When you reach this point, you may be doing a number of theme-related, technology-integrated units of study. The balance of whole-group involvement, small-group activities, and individual pursuits seems natural and you are maximizing use of the technology at your disposal. The software available to you has enabled you to individualize students' programs and you have a clear understanding of the different strengths and weaknesses of each child. Your evaluation methods have grown to include not only teacher evaluation, but also peer and self-evaluation, and you are gathering individual portfolios on each student.

> ## A Teacher's Diary
> I find the classroom very hectic and the noise level higher than I had anticipated. I'm having a hard time reassuring myself that everyone is really working and I'm feeling particularly concerned about the productivity of a few students who have difficulty staying on-task. I think I'll pull the whole group back together tomorrow — re-teach some concepts and review some routines. Then we'll try again in a few days.

Continue reading and participating in workshops. By now, you have probably established and realized the value of your support group. Ongoing communication with the administration and parent community is also important. If you were to reflect on the physical arrangement of your classroom when you first started, you may realize that it looks very different today. Gone are the rows of desks, replaced by more flexible arrangements and workstations that vary according to needs. Paper and pencil are no longer the only way of completing assignments; now, students have a variety of resources right at their fingertips through which they can pursue group and individual challenges.

> ## A Teacher's Diary
> It's amazing how independent my students are becoming. They are responding well and are so motivated by their assignments. I never realized how much I would have to change my strategies for teaching and evaluating. What I like about the program is that there is lots of room for initiative and personal contact. Everyone is excited, including me.

Refinement

You are ready to refine your technological classroom. You may be looking for additional resources that can better perform certain functions, or ways to use your existing resources more effectively.

You feel comfortable creating your own theme-related units that incorporate technology and address different rates and styles of learning. It is not unusual for you to involve your students in this process and you are always open to new and more effective ways of doing things.

A Teacher's Diary

I'm pleased with the thinking and processes that I see going on in my classroom but I'm concerned that the final products my students are turning in are not of the quality I would like. We need to look for some better ways of combining media. I'm wondering if a more sophisticated multimedia platform is available and affordable. I'll discuss it with my principal and the technology consultant.

Evaluation

This is the stage at which you assess what you have accomplished, including the design of the curriculum, the way in which it has been implemented, and the effectiveness of the technology in achieving your desired goals. The focus of the technology-oriented classroom revolves around the needs of the individual students. You explore new ways of writing assignments, using the technology and resources, and evaluating learning outcomes. All those involved in the innovation come together to establish new goals and a corresponding action plan that will again challenge both teacher and students.

A Teacher's Diary

I think I've made some really good progress this year in integrating computers and other technology in my classroom. We need to make a school plan so that I can move ahead next year with something new. I'm ready to tackle tele-communications so that my students can get more instant information and we can communicate with other students and teachers. How can I get a modem and access a network? Maybe we can plan some fund-raising or explore connections to business through some of our parents.

Progress through these stages is not always smooth or easy; you are sure to encounter some obstacles along the way. By identifying potential barriers before you actually face them, you are able to develop strategies for overcoming them instead of letting them defeat you.

Strategic School Technology Planning

A well-developed plan that addresses why existing technology has not been well utilized; how learning resource management could be improved; who would be responsible for what aspects of the plan in the future; and how the school could evaluate its progress toward technology integration provides powerful support for the effective use of technology.[1]

A school technology plan must be a strategic plan, including not only what will be done, but also how it will be accomplished. The plan needs to be flexible enough to accommodate fiscal uncertainty, while still reflecting the school's vision.

Think of technology in relation to curriculum, as a part of the curriculum delivery system. The purchase of technology is just as important as the purchase of pencils and books. What are the needs of students and teachers? What will the technology enable them to do? How will the use of this technology enhance or change existing curricula?

A committee of curriculum and technology specialists can help you to clarify some of these issues. Knowledge of the change process will assist the committee members as they plan for the simultaneous introduction of technology and pedagogical innovation.

A school plan should include:

- names of school planning committee members;
- objectives of the school planning committee;
- school philosophy regarding technology use;
- technology currently belonging to the school;
- current technology usage and scheduling;
- proposed changes to current technology usage and scheduling;
- hardware/software purchase plan, including items to be purchased, proposed year of purchase, cost, and source of funds (include grants, donations);
- budget for support materials such as paper, disks, printer cartridges;
- source and cost of technical support (maintenance, repairs, and upgrades);
- roles of principal, teachers, specialists;
- professional development plan for teachers;
- partnerships established or to be pursued with businesses;
- security;
- specific recommendations, initiatives, and priorities for the present year;
- annual evaluation and review date.

Gone are the days of technology plans that specify computer skills for students, such as how to program in BASIC or load and run programs. Research and practice have shown that technology plans are not effective unless they are tied to school-wide efforts for educational improvement.[2]

Glossary of Technological and Pedagogical Terms

activity-based learning Learning that involves the active participation of the student.

application software A computer program written for a particular purpose; examples include word processing, spreadsheet, database.

assessment The process of data collection. A variety of alternative forms of assessment exist, including tests, portfolios, peer evaluation, daily work, self-evaluation.

bar codes Groups of optically coded parallel lines, such as those seen on grocery items. Used to convey or access information in a number of areas (e.g., accessing videodisc screens).

baud rate The rate of speed (bits per second) at which information is transferred via modem over telephone lines. Most computer telecommunications take place at 2400, 4800, or 9600 baud.

benchmarks Objectives that students master consistently.

bookmark A marker in an electronic document/software program. The use of bookmarks during the viewing of a videodisc or CD-ROM allows the student to tag key points and return to them at a later time.

boot The process of loading the operating system of a computer.

bug An error in a computer program. It prevents the computer from doing what the programer has instructed it to do.

bulletin board (electronic) An electronic version of the familiar community bulletin board. With a computer, a modem, a telephone line, and communications software, users can see the information on the board and record their new input.

camcorder A video camera and videotape recorder as a single unit.

CD-ROM (Compact disc–read-only memory) Information that has been permanently recorded on a compact disc. CD-ROM discs are smaller than videodiscs. With the discs and a microcomputer, students can experience interactive instruction.

central processing unit See **CPU**.

chips Small rectangular pieces, usually silicone, inside a microcomputer that contain electrical circuits.

clip art Predrawn artwork that can be imported from a computer program and integrated into the user's work. A wide variety of clip-art packages, such as cartoons, animals, people, and designs, can be purchased for use on personal computers.

cognitive skills Thought processes involved in learning. They are skills involved in the acquisition, application, and manipulation of information.

computer system The components necessary to carry out computer tasks. A basic computer system typically has a CPU (central processing unit), a keyboard, a monitor, disk drives, and a printer.

cooperative learning A small group of learners working purposefully and actively together on specific tasks.

copy-protected Diskette that cannot be copied by ordinary means.

CPU A computer's central processing unit. It is a hardware component and is responsible for taking information from the computer's memory, determining what needs to be done, and directing the necessary action.

cursor The prompting symbol displayed on the monitor that shows where the next character will appear.

cyberspace The conceptual world of individuals and organizations accessible through a computer network.

database A collection of related data organized to address the information needs of a variety of users.

database software A program that allows the user to access and manage data.

desktop publishing software Special computer software for creating and laying out pages of text and graphics.

disk drive A mechanical device, part of a computer system, capable of reading from and writing to a disk.

dot matrix printer A printer that produces a printout by printing a series of dots to form letters. This type of printer is relatively inexpensive. See **ink-jet printer** and **laser printer**.

download Occurs when you receive a file from a remote computer.

electronic bulletin board An electronic communication system that allows the users to share and transfer information.

electronic conferencing A conference arranged by electronically connecting individuals or groups.

electronic mail Also known as e-mail; letters, messages, etc., sent through a computer network from office to office or organization to organization by electronic means. It is like having your own private mailbox.

e-mail See **electronic mail**.

feedback Information that provides a response based on the user's activity. Many software packages provide the user with immediate feedback in the form of check marks or comments such as "OK," "Good," "Try again."

fileserver The computer in any network that acts as the repository of files that can be used by other nodes in the network.

floppy disk	An electromagnetic storage device on which information is stored for transfer to the computer's RAM (random access memory; see **RAM**). Floppies come in two basic diameters: 5.25 inch and 3.5 inch.
font	A description of a character of type.
formative assessment	Assessment that is ongoing and that views learning as a continuous process.
hardware	A general term for the equipment that comprises a computer system, such as a computer, fileserver, printer, etc.
hypermedia	Type of software consisting of networks of text, graphics, audio and/or video clips.
icon	A small picture that replaces a text command on the screen.
individualized learning	The tailoring of teaching and learning to meet the needs of the individual student.
ink-jet printer	Also known as a bubble-jet printer. A printer that produces a printout by spraying droplets of ink onto paper. Quieter but more expensive than dot matrix printers.
input	Information that is sent to the computer's memory. Inputting usually occurs via the keyboard, storage disk, or modem.
integration	The linking of specific components. When technology is integrated into the curriculum, it becomes an essential part of the delivery system.
interactive videodisc	An optical disc capable of storing and playing back still frames or motion video and two channels of audio by means of a videodisc player. It is approximately equivalent to 500 floppy disks.
jack	A receptacle for a plug for input or output for audio or video.
joystick	A handle attached to a square or rectangular platform that allows the user to control movement on the screen.
LAN	A local area network, usually within one building. A central processor controls the activities of a number of microcomputers.
laser printer	A high-speed, high-quality printer that uses some form of electrophotography to produce print. Laser printers are more costly than dot matrix or ink-jet printers, but the quality of product is superior.
LCD panel	A liquid crystal display panel or tablet, usually used in conjunction with a computer and overhead projector to display computer images on a projection screen.
learning styles	Different ways of learning, frequently referred to as learning preferences.
local area network	See **LAN**.
login	A signing-on procedure. Special logins allow users to secure their work. Students should be cautioned to never use another student's login.
Logo	A simple, powerful programming language designed for use by young students. It is not platform-specific.

manipulative materials Student learning resources such as geoboards, tangrams, blocks, magnets, modeling clay, centicubes, beakers, spring scales, etc.

modem Abbreviation of modulator/demodulator. The device is attached between the telephone line and the computer so that the computer can send digital information over telephone lines to other computers that have modems; hardware for transferring information from one computer to another via telephone lines.

monitor (computer) The display unit that is connected to the computer system. Monitors come in two basic types: monochrome and color.

monitoring Carrying out an ongoing assessment.

mouse A hand-operated device for controlling the movement of the cursor on the computer screen. It is connected to the computer by a cable.

multimedia A computer-based system that allows students to access, control, and organize information in a variety of ways, using graphics, text, animation, video, and audio. It provides links that connect facts, ideas, words, and pictures.

networked computers A system consisting of a number of interconnected computers that are capable of sharing information.

off-line Not hooked up to a central computer or a network by telephone line.

on-line In direct contact with a central computer or a network.

operating system Special software instructions to the computer that help it to interpret what other software is doing. Operating systems determine how to get information from disks, what to do with it, and how to put it back.

output Information sent out of the computer to printer, modem.

pedagogy The practice or profession of teaching.

peer evaluation Assessment made by a student of similar age.

peripherals Equipment that attaches to computers, such as printers, videodisc players, or CD-ROM drives. These transfer information to and from the computer.

program Set of instructions stored in the computer that tells the computer what activities to perform.

RAM Acronym for random access memory; the memory that stores the current program. The contents change when a new program is run. Information in RAM usually disappears when the computer is turned off.

resolution The degree to which detail can be shown. It is measured in dots vertically and horizontally.

robotics Deals with the design, capabilities, and uses of robots.

ROM Acronym for read-only memory. It is the permanent part of the computer's memory. Information can be read but not changed.

scanner A device that uses light to scan pictures, graphs, etc., and sends the information to the computer to be stored on disk and reproduced on screen.

simulation	A representation of the real event or process. Simulation software can show, for example, the effect of light and water on plant growth, the prey/predator relationship and its impact on the balance of nature, or the effect of the removal of oxygen on a flame.
software	See **program**.
spreadsheet	A computer program that generates and operates complete tables of data, information, etc. Inputting of mathematical formulas allows changes in one area to be reflected in changes to other items.
stand-alone computer	A computer used independently of a network.
summative evaluation	A type of evaluation tihat provides a clear perception of a student's knowledge and skills after a specific period of time.
teacher utility	A program specifically designed for teachers that enables them to accomplish one or more education-related tasks efficiently.
telecommunications	The communication that occurs between computers via telephone lines and modems. Special software is required.
teleconferencing	Communication using voice with still frames or motion video, made possible by telephone lines or satellite technology.
VCR	A videocassette recorder that records and plays back visual images and sound.
videoconferencing	Using a computer, telephone, and video technology to allow people at different locations to converse on-screen and also exchange visual information.
videodisc	A disc on which visual images with or without sound are recorded. On CLV (constant linear velocity) discs, data is stored in one long track. CLV discs are relatively inexpensive. On CAV (constant angular velocity) discs, data is stored on a series of rings on a disc. These discs are more expensive than the CLV variety but are more versatile.
videodisc player	The equipment that enables the user to play a videodisc, either through the VCR or a computer.
virtual classroom	A setting that maximizes the opportunities for learning made available by telecommunications systems, providing learners with access to resources throughout the world. The virtual classroom provides for technological enhancement of the educational curriculum, including access to courses, mentors, and experts through networked resources.
virtual reality	The display and control of a simulated environment into which a user enters and moves around, interacting with objects. The user may use datagloves, datasuit, or a helmet.
word processing software	A computer program that allows the user to enter, edit, save, and print text.

References

CHAPTER 1 Why Integrate Technology into the Classroom?

1. Daniels, H., M. Kaufman, G. Meo, J. Naylor, and E. Whelihan. "Planning for technology: Circa 1992." *SIGTC Connections,* vol. 8, no. 4, 1992, p. 29.

2. Daggett, W. *Elementary/Middle School Presentation* (video). Schenectady, NY: International Center for Leadership in Education, 1992.

3. Bransford, J.D., R.D. Sherwood, T.S. Hasselbring, C.K. Kinzer, and S.M. Williams. *Anchored Instruction: Why We Need It and How Technology Can Help Cognition, Education and Multimedia: Exploring Ideas in High Technology.* Hillsdale, NJ: Lawrence Erlbaum, 1990, pp. 115-141.

4. DeWitt, J. "Computers pay off by curbing dropout rate." *The Electronic School,* September 1989, pp. A22-A23.

5. Carmichael, H.W., J.D. Burnett, W.C. Higginson, B.G. Moore, and D.J. Dollard. *Computers, children and classrooms: A multi-site evaluation of the creative use of microcomputers by elementary school children.* Ontario Ministry of Education. Toronto: Queen's Printer of Ontario, 1985.

   Robertson, E.B., B.H. Ladewig, M.P. Strickland, and M.D Boschuna, "Enhancement of self-esteem through the use of computer-assisted instruction." *Journal of Educational Research,* vol. 80, no. 5, 1987, pp. 314-316.

   Sturtevant, M. "Computers more than a teaching tool." *FWTAO Newsletter,* vol. 9, no. 2, 1990, pp. 32-34.

6. Mevarech, Z.R., and Y. Rich. "Effects of computer-assisted mathematics instruction on disadvantaged children's cognitive and affective development." *Journal of Educational Research*, vol. 79, no. 1, 1985, pp. 5-11.

7. Ibid.

   Robertson, E.B., B.H. Ladewig, M.P. Strickland, and M.D. Boschuna. "Enhancement of self-esteem through the use of computer-assisted instruction." *Journal of Educational Research,* vol. 80, no. 5, 1987, pp. 314-316.

   Trifiletti, J., G.H. Firth, and S. Armstrong. "Microcomputers versus resource rooms for learning disabled students: A preliminary investigation of the effects on mathematics skills." *Learning Disability Quarterly*, vol. 7, no. 1, 1984, pp. 69-76.

8. Tierney, R. "The influence of immediate computer access on students' thinking." *Apple Classrooms of Tomorrow*, Report #3, 1989.

9. Dalton, D.W., and M.J. Hannafin. "The effects of computer-assisted and traditional mastery methods on computation accuracy and attitudes." *Journal of Educational Research*, vol. 82, no. 1, 1988, p. 32.

10. Sculley, J. *Odyssey*. New York: Harper & Row, 1987, p. 362.

11. Horowitz, R.A. "Effects of the 'open' classroom." In H.J. Walberg (ed.), *Educational Environments and Effects*. Berkley, CA: McCutchan, 1979, p. 4.

    Walberg, H.J. "Synthesis of research on teaching." In M.C. Wittrofck (ed.), *Handbook of Research on Teaching* (3rd ed.). New York: MacMillan, 1986.

    Weeks, R.C. "Activity-based learning: In search of a definition and a related study." Paper presented at the 33rd Annual Conference of the Ontario Educational Research Council, Toronto, ON, Dec. 6-7, 1991.

12. Gersten, R.M., W.C. Becker, T.J. Heiry, and W.A.White. "Entry IQ and yearly academic growth of children in direct instructional programs: A longitudinal study of low SES children." *Educational Evaluation and Policy Analysis 6*, 1984, pp. 109-121.

    Olstad, R. G., and D.L. Haury. "A summary of research in science education: 1982." *Science Education*, vol. 68, 1984, pp. 207-363.

13. Mevarech, Z.R., and Y. Rich. "Effects of computer-assisted mathematics instruction on disadvantaged children's cognitive and affective development." *Journal of Educational Research*, vol. 79, no. 1, 1985, pp. 5-11.

    Terwell, J. "Implementation and effects of a program for mixed ability teaching in secondary mathematics education." Paper presented at the Annual Conference of the American Educational Research Association, New Orleans, LA, April 5-9, 1988.

14. Fulton, M.L. "Increasing third grade social skills through co-operative learning techniques." Unpublished practicum, Nova University, Fort Lauderdale, FL, 1990.

    Mevarech, Z.R., and Y. Rich. "Effects of computer-assisted mathematics instruction on disadvantaged children's cognitive and affective development." *Journal of Educational Research*, vol. 79, no.1, 1985, pp. 5-11.

15. Madden, N.A., R.J. Stevens, and R.E. Slavin. "Reading instruction in the mainstream: A cooperative learning approach." *Report #5*. Baltimore, MD: Centre for Research on Elementary and Middle Schools, 1986.

16. Terwell, J. "Implementation and effects of a program for mixed ability teaching in secondary mathematics education." Paper presented at the Annual Conference of the American Educational Research Association, New Orleans, LA, April 5-9, 1988.

17. Brennan, J. "We must compute." *The Ottawa Citizen*, Oct.18, 1992, p. B1.

18. Borrell, J. "America's shame: How we've abandoned our children's future." *MacWorld*, September 30, 1992, p. 30.

19. Corcoran, Elizabeth. "Why kids love computer nets." *Fortune*, Sept. 1993, pp.103-108.

20. Braun, L. "School dropouts, economics and technology." *The Computing Teacher*, vol. 18, no. 6, 1991, pp. 24-25.

21. Canadian Corporate Council on Education. *Employability Skills Profile*. Ottawa, ON: The Conference Board of Canada, 1992.

22. Decker, R., and R.J. Krajewski. "The role of technology in education: High schools of the future." *NASSP Bulletin*, November 1985.

23. Shann, M.H. "Curriculum integration using computers as tools for learning." *SIGTC Connections*, vol. 8, no. 3, 1992, p. 7.

24. White, M.A. "A curriculum for the information age." *Technology in Today's Schools*. Cynthia Warger (ed), Association for Supervision and Curriculum Development, 1990, p. 9.

25. Ely, D.P. "Trends and issues in educational technology." *Educational Media and Technology Yearbook*. Littleton, CO: Libraries Unlimited Inc., 1990, p. 16.

26. Drucker, P. *The New Realities*. New York: Harper & Row, 1989, p. 249.

CHAPTER 2   Where Are You Going?

1. Peters, T., and N. Austin. *A Passion for Excellence*. New York: Warner Books, 1985, p. 486.

2. Maddux, C.D., D.L. Johnson, and J.N. Willis. *Educational computing: Learning with tomorrow's technologies*. Boston: Allyn & Bacon, 1992.

3. Green, B.M. *Great workshops*. Watertown, MA: Tom Snyder Productions, 1990, p. 43.

4. Stone, A. "Action for equity." *The Computing Teacher*, vol. 14, no. 3, p. 54.

5. Fullan, M. "Change processes and strategies at the local level." *The Elementary School Journal*, vol. 85, no. 3, 1985, pp. 391-420.

   ———. "Curriculum implementation." *The International Encylopedia of Educational Technology*. New York: Pergamon Press, 1989, pp. 485–491.

   ———. *The meaning of educational change*. Toronto, ON: OISE Press and Teachers College Press, 1982.

   Leithwood, K.A., and D.J. Montgomery. *A framework for planned educational change: Application to the assessment of program implementation*. Toronto, ON: The Ontario Institute for Studies in Education, 1981.

   Wright, R. "A contextual model of curriculum implementation." Thesis (Ph.D.), University of Ottawa, Ottawa, ON, 1982.

6. Ibid.

7. Ibid.

8. Milheim, W.D. "Linking education and industry: Reasons for mutual cooperation." *Tech Trends*, vol. 36, no. 4, 1991, pp. 15-18.

9. "The call to partnerships." *Becoming Partners*. Cupertino, CA: Apple Computer Inc., 1992, p. A6.

10. Tolbert, T.L. "Industry access to university technology: Prospects and problems." In E.J. Friese (ed.), *The private sector/university technology alliance: Making it work*. Proceeding of a conference of the National Council of University Research Administrators, Dallas, TX, Sept. 1984, pp. 24-28.

CHAPTER 3   What About Equipment?

1. Hayes, J. (ed). *Microcomputer and VCR Usage in Schools*. Denver, CO: Quality Education Data Inc., 1988, p. 78.

2. Skolnik, R., A. Larson, and C. Smith. "The power of multimedia." *The Electronic School*, September 1993, p. A7.

3. Ibid., p. A8.

4. Ryba, K., and B. Anderson. *Learning with Computers: Effective Teaching Strategies*. Eugene, OR: The International Society for Technology in Education, 1990, p. 71.

5. Harasim, L. "Learning to teach online." *Telecommunications in Education News*, vol. 5, no. 1, 1993, p. 24.

6. Burge, E.J., and J.M. Roberts. *Classrooms with a Difference: A Practical Guide to the Use of Conferencing Technologies*. Toronto, ON: The Ontario Institute for Studies in Education, 1993.

7. November, A., and D. Thornburg. "Telecom: The good, the bad and the ugly." *Electronic Learning*, vol. 12, no. 7, 1993, pp. 16-17.

8. Kearns, K. "The forgotten medium – Are we too visually dependent?" *NASSP Bulletin*, vol. 69, no. 480, 1985, pp. 45-49.

9. Jukes, I. "Electronic highways for tomorrow: Paradigm and change." Presentation to the Educational Computing Organization of Ontario, Toronto, ON, May 1993.

CHAPTER 4 Making It Work

1. Tucker, R.N. "Transitions in European education." *The Interactive Learning Revolution: Multimedia in Education and Training*. New York: Nicols Publishing, 1990, p. 44.

2. Komoski, P.K. "Educational computing: The burden of ensuring quality." *Phi Delta Kappan*, December 1984, pp. 244-248.

3. Geisert, P.G., and M.K. Futrell. *Teachers, computers and curriculum*. Boston: Allyn & Bacon, 1990.

4. Leventhal, S., M. Melton, and P. Stevens. "Managing data demons." Paper presented at 10th International Conference on Technology in Education. Boston, MA, March 1993, p. 1.

5. Ryba, K., and B. Anderson. *Learning with Computers: Effective Teaching Strategies*. Eugene, OR: The International Society for Technology in Education, 1990.

6. Watson, J. "Cooperative learning and computers: One way to address student differences." *The Computing Teacher*, vol. 18, no. 4, 1990-91, pp. 5-8.

7. Bruder, I. "Multimedia: How It Changes the Way We Teach and Learn." *Electronic Learning*, September 1991, pp. 22-26.

8. Roden, S. "Multimedia: The future of training." *UltiMedia Digest*, vol. 1, 1991, p. 80.

9. D'Ignazio, F. "Illumination – It's elementary!" *The Computing Teacher*, 1993, vol. 21, no. 2, pp. 53-55.

10. ————. "Student multimedia book talks: Illuminating on a shoestring." *The Computing Teacher*, vol. 21, no. 3, 1993, p. 32.

11. Kurshan, B. "Telecommunications in the classroom." *The Computing Teacher*, vol. 17, no. 7, 1990, p. 30.

12. Ibid.

13. Riel, M. *Telecommunications: A tool reconnecting kids with society*. Report prepared for the AT & T Long Distance Learning Network, 1989.

14. Levin, J.A., A. Rogers, M.L. Waugh, and K. Smith. "Electronic networks: Appropriate activities for learning." *The Computing Teacher*, vol. 16, no. 8, 1989, pp. 17-21.

15. Newman, D., and F. Torz. "*The world in the classroom: Interacting with data from outside the school*." Paper presented at the American Educational Research Association, Boston, MA, April 1990.

16. Brehm, B. "The places project: Cooperative learning, problem solving, and telecommunications to enhance learning." *Telecommunications in Education News*, vol. 4, no. 3-4, 1993, pp. 6-7.

17. Clark, D., as quoted in "Why kids love computer nets." *Fortune*, September 1993, p. 108.

18. Wilson, S., as quoted in "Why kids love computer nets." *Fortune*, September 1993, p. 108.

19. Rogers, A., Y. Andres, M. Jacks, and T. Claustel. "Keys to successful telecommunications." *Electronic Learning*, vol. 11, no. 6, 1992, p. 19.

20. Brehm, B. "The places project: Cooperative learning, problem solving, and telecommunications to enhance learning." *Telecommunications in Education News*, vol. 4, no. 3-4, 1993, pp. 6-7.

21. Botterbusch, H.R. "Tune-In and Turn On! Videos in the Classroom." *Tech Trends*, vol. 36, no. 4, 1991, pp. 22-24.

22. *The Videodisc Compendium*. St. Paul, MN: Emerging Technology Consultants Inc., 1991-92.

23. Pollack, R.A. "The state of videodiscs in education and training." *Instructional Delivery Systems*, vol. 4, no. 1, 1990, pp. 12-14.

24. Dockterman, D. *Great Teaching and the VCR*. Watertown, MA: Tom Snyder Productions, 1993, p. 5.

CHAPTER 5   What About Curriculum?

1. Zorfass, J. "Curriculum: A critical factor in technology integration." *The Computing Teacher*, February 1993, p. 14.

2. Caissy, G.A. "Planning for Computer Use in the Classroom." *Computers in Education*, March 1988, p. 10.

3. Glasser, W. *Control theory in the classroom*. New York: Harper & Row, 1986.

4. Zorfass, J. "Curriculum: A critical factor in technology integration." *The Computing Teacher*, February 1993, p. 14.

CHAPTER 6   Getting Started

1. Sculley, J. *Odyssey*. New York: Harper & Row, 1987, pp. 401-402.

2. Solomon, G. "Technology and the balance of power." *The Computing Teacher*, vol. 19, no. 8, 1992, p. 10.

3. Church, E. "Shopping for educational software." *The Globe and Mail*, April 15, 1993, p. C1.

CHAPTER 7   The Well-Mannered, Safe, Technological Classroom

1. Frost, S. "Computer-mediated learning: A necessity in the elementary classroom?" *Output*, vol. 3, no. 2, 1992, pp. 14-19.

2. Yoder, S. "Ergonomics forgotten or are we teaching carpel tunnel syndrome?" *The Computing Teacher*, vol. 21, no. 4, 1993-94, pp. 30-31.

CHAPTER 8   Evaluating Student Progress

1. Herman, J., P.R. Aschbacher, and L.A.Winters. *A Practical Guide to Alternative Assessment*. Alexandria, VA: Association for Supervision and Curriculum Development, 1992, p. V.

2. *In Common*, vol. 1, no. 2, 1993. Toronto, ON: Ministry of Education and Training, Ontario.

3. White, M. A. "Current trends in education and technology as signs of the future." *Education & Computing 5*, proceedings from the Conference on Educational Software at Reykjavik, Iceland, June 18-22, 1989, p. 5.

4. Ryba, K., and B. Anderson. *Learning with computers: Effective teaching strategies*. Eugene, OR: International Society for Technology in Education, 1990, p. 26.

5. White, M.A. "Current trends in education and technology as signs of the future." *Education and Computing 5*, proceedings from the Conference on Educational Software at Reykjavik, Iceland, June 18-22, 1989, pp. 3-10.

CHAPTER 9   Students with Special Needs

1. Watson, J. "Cooperative learning and computers: One way to address student differences." *The Computing Teacher*, Dec./Jan. 1991-92, p. 9.

2. Hannaford, A.E., and F.M. Taber. "Microcomputer software for the handicapped: Development and evaluation." *Exceptional Children*, vol. 49, no. 2, 1982, pp. 13-14.

3. Costanzo, W. *The Electronic Text: Learning to Read, Write and Reason with Computers*. Englewood Cliffs, NJ: Educational Technology Publications, 1989.

   Krendl, K.A., and D.A. Lieberman. "Computers and learning: A review of recent research." *Journal of Educational Computing Research*, vol. 4, no. 4, 1988, pp. 367-389.

   Fisher, G. "The social effects of computers in education." *Electronic Learning*, March 1984, pp. 26-28.

4. Watson, J. "Cooperative learning and computers: One way to address student differences." *The Computing Teacher*, Dec./Jan. 1991-92, pp. 5-8.

5. Ibid. p. 5.

6. *Becoming Partners. A guide to starting and sustaining successful partnerships between education and business*. Cupertino, CA: Apple Computer Inc., p. A45.

7. McVicar, J. *Towards Enabling All Learners: Computer-based Technology for Students with Special Needs*. Education Technology Centre of British Columbia, 1991, p. 3. The quotation at the end is from: Morocco, C., and J. Zorfass. "Technology and transformation: A naturalistic study of special students and computers in middle school." *Journal of Special Education Technology*, vol. 9, no. 2, 1988, pp. 88-97.

8. Speziale, M.L., and L.M. La France. "Multimedia students with learning disabilities: The road to success." *The Computing Teacher*, vol. 20, no. 3, 1992, p. 31.

9. Sturtevant, M. "Computers more than a teaching tool." *FWTAO Newsletter*, vol. 9, no. 2, 1990, pp. 32-34.

10. Witchita, KS, Public School Board motto, 1993.

11. Norris, C. "Computing and the Classroom: Teaching the At-Risk Student." *The Computing Teacher*, vol. 21, no. 5, 1994, p. 12.

CHAPTER 10 **Tools for Teachers**

1. Kelman, P. "Alternatives to Integrated Instructional Systems." Paper presented at the National Educational Computing Conference, Nashville, TN, June 1990, p. 89.

2. November, A., and D. Thornburg. "Telecom: The good, the bad and the ugly." *Electronic Learning*, vol. 12, no. 7, 1993, pp. 16-17.

3. *Power On! New Tools for Teaching and Learning.* Washington, DC: Congress of the United States, Office of Technology Assessment, 1988, p. 89.

4. Beaver, J.F. "Using computer power to improve your teaching (Part One)." *Output*, vol. 14, no. 3, 1994, p. 25.

5. D'Ignazio, F. "Welcome to the multimedia sandbox." *The Computing Teacher*, vol. 17, no. 1, 1989, pp. 27-28.

6. Howles, L., and C. Pettengill. "Designing an instructional multimedia presentation: A seven-step process." *Journal of Hypermedia and Multimedia Studies*, vol. 3, no. 4. 1993, pp. 6-9. Eugene, OR: International Society for Technology in Education.

7. McCarthy, R. "A computer on every teacher's desk." *Electronic Learning*, vol. 12, no. 7, 1993, p. 10.

8. "Opportunities: Teacher productivity." *Becoming Partners – A guide to starting and sustaining successful partnerships between education and business.* Cupertino, California: Apple Computer Inc., 1992, p. A39.

9. Kerr, J., and J. Radue. "Online." *Output*, vol. 14, no. 3, 1994, p. 29.

10. Fletcher, S. "Using a data base in an elementary school." *Computers in Education*, April 1988, p. 10.

11. Fox, R.G. "Let's teach our teachers about computers." Society for Applied Learning Technology Newsletter, Fall, 1988, p. 1.

12. Tracy, B. As cited in "Raw material of information age is knowledge" by Janis Foord Kirk in *The Toronto Star*, Nov. 20, 1993, p. G7.

13. Ibid.

14. Morgan, B. (ed.). "101 things you want to know about educational technology." *Electronic Learning*, vol. 10, no. 7, 1991, p. 25.

Toward the Future

1. Thornburg, D. *Education Technology and Paradigms of Change for the 21st Century.* Starsong Publications, 1989, p. 111.

2. Jukes, I. "Electronic highways for tomorrow: Paradigm and change." Presentation at the Educational Computing Organization of Ontario, Toronto, ON, 1993.

3. D'Ignazio, F. "Beyond multimedia: The student as Sherlock Holmes." *The Computing Teacher*, vol. 21, no. 5, 1994, p. 40.

Appendix 1

[2]Leithwood, K.A., and D.J. Montgomery. *A framework for planned educational change: Application to the assessment of program implementation.* Toronto, ON: The Ontario Institute for Studies in Education, 1981.

Appendix 2

1. Wiburg, K. "Integrating technologies into schools: Why has it been so slow?" *The Computing Teacher*, vol. 21, no. 5, p. 7.
2. Ibid.

Other References

Abrami, P. C. et al. *Using Cooperative Learning*. Montreal, PQ: Centre for the Study of Classroom Processes, Concordia University, 1993.

Bahnuik, R., and P. Ponting. "The chat mode in the elementary classroom." *Computers in Education*, vol. 5, no. 8, 1988, pp. 30-31.

Bitter, G. *Microcomputers in Education Today*. Watsonville, CA: Mitchell Publishing Inc., 1989.

Bullough, R.V., and L. F. Beatty. *Classroom Applications of Microcomputers* (2nd ed.). New York: Macmillan Publishing Co., 1991.

Erekson, T., and L. Barr. "New directions for business education curriculum." *NASSP Bulletin*, November 1985, pp. 25-28.

Finkel, L. "Planning for obsolescence." *Electronic Learning*, vol. 12, no. 7, 1993, pp. 18-19.

Goodlad, J. *The Dynamics of Educational Change*. Toronto, ON: McGraw-Hill, 1975.

Grandgenett, N., and K. Sullivan. "Troubleshooting the classroom microcomputer." *The Computing Teacher*, vol. 17, no. 6, 1990, pp. 36-39.

Hall, G., and S. Loucks. "Levels of use of the innovation: A framework for analyzing innovation adoption." *Journal of Teacher Education*, vol. 24, no. 1, 1975, pp. 5-7.

Hill, M. "Math reform: No technology, no chance." *Electronic Learning*, vol. 12, no. 7, 1993, pp. 24-32.

Hoy, W.K., and C.G. Miskel. *Educational Administration*. New York: Random House Inc., 1987.

Kaufman, D., M. Mco, G. Maylor, and E. Whelihan. "Planning for technology: Circa 1992." *SIGTC Connections*, vol. 8, no. 4, 1992, pp. 29-31.

Killian, J. E., and L.J. McClure. "Computers, language arts and change: South Illinois University's Teacher Renewal Institute." *Journal of Computing in Teacher Education*, vol. 9, no. 1, 1992, pp. 13-19.

LeBaron, J. "Grab your partner." *Electronic Learning*, vol. 10, no. 1, 1990, p. 18.

Mojkowski, C. "Technology and curriculum: Will the promised revolution take place?" *NASSP Bulletin*, February 1987, pp. 113-118.

Stephenson, C. "An interview with Sharon McCoy Bell." *The Computing Teacher*, vol. 21, no. 5, 1994, pp. 9-11.

Truett, C. "CD-ROM comes of age in the high school media center: Teaching research skills." *The Computing Teacher*, vol. 17, no. 5, 1990, pp. 39-41.

Vatrma, I. "One computer in a classroom." *SIGTC Connections*, vol. 8, no. 3, 1992, pp. 13-15.

Wasylenki, L. "Using hypercard in the classroom." *Computers in Education*, vol. 6, no. 2, pp. 8-9.

Magazine references

Computers in Education
Moorshead Publications Ltd.
1300 Don Mills Road
North York, Ontario
M3B 3M8
Telephone (416) 445-5600   Fax (416) 445-8149

The Computing Teacher
International Society for Technology in Education
1787 Agate Street
Eugene, OR 97403-1923
Telephone (503) 346-4414   Fax (503) 346-5890

Electronic Learning
Scholastic Inc.
730 Broadway, New York, NY 10003-9538
Telephone (212) 505-4900   Fax (212) 260-8611

Teaching and Computers
Scholastic Inc.
730 Broadway, New York, NY 10003-9538
Telephone (212) 505-3482

Technology and Learning
Peter Li Inc.
330 Progress Road
Dayton, OH 45449
Telephone (513) 847-5900